Adventures
of an
Italian Food
Lover

Adventures of an Italian Food Lover

WITH RECIPES FROM 254 OF MY VERY BEST FRIENDS

Faith Heller Willinger

Watercolors by Suzanne Heller

CLARKSON POTTER/PUBLISHERS
NEW YORK

Published in the United States by Clarkson Potter/Publishers, an imprint of the
Crown Publishing Group, a division of Random House, Inc., New York.
www.crownpublishing.com
www.clarksonpotter.com

Clarkson N. Potter is a trademark and Potter and colophon are registered
trademarks of Random House, Inc.

Library of Congress Cataloging-in-Publication Data
Willinger, Faith Heller.
    Adventures of an Italian food lover / Faith Heller Willinger.
    Includes index.
1. Cookery, Italian.   I. Title.
TX723.W565   2007
641.5945—dc22   2007003885

ISBN 978-0-307-34639-1

Printed in the United States of America

Design by Maggie Hinders

10   9   8   7   6   5   4   3   2   1

First Edition

CONTENTS

'M LUCKY. I live in Italy. For the past thirty years I've lived in Florence, where I'm happily married to a Florentine Etruscan engineer with an impeccable palate, and I've raised my son, Max. I also have the best job in the world, writing about Italian food, wine, and travel. I'm obsessed with these pursuits—and so are most Italians.

My husband refers to me as the samurai shopper, or the vegetable warrior. I was raised to shop for clothes, shoes, accessories, coordinated outfits. I collected modern art. When I abandoned my previous existence, moved to Italy, and got passionate about cooking, I studied with Andreas Hellrigl, a master chef in Merano, Alto Adige, who later moved to New York and created the food at Palio. He was an inspiration, showing me what grand cuisine was all about. Andreas introduced me to real balsamic vinegar, Carnaroli rice, super-fresh fish, quality meats and poultry; the finest *salumi,* cheeses, and wines; the most interesting kitchen equipment. I transferred my shopping skills from art collecting and the wardrobe to the kitchen, tracking down the very best ingredients and tools I could get my hands on. I frequent the Santo Spirito vegetable stands when they open at 7:30 A.M. because I want first choice of the best produce. Now my passion for all things culinary has taken me all over the country, from the Alps to islands off the coast of Sicily, tracking down the best restaurants, wine makers, and food artisans, while visiting Italy's artistic and architectural wonders and shopping between meals. I go to trade fairs and conferences. I've hung out in kitchens, wood-burning bread bakeries, wine cellars, butcher shops, dairies, farms, and markets. I've spent time and calories at the table, and traveled the back roads to reach towns most people have never heard of. I've learned fish names in local dialects, visited a truffle market in Piemonte at dawn, attended a wholesale fish auction in Venice, watched artisans at work all over Italy. Along the way I've made lots of friends. They've introduced me to their friends, I've introduced them to mine. Now in turn I'd like to introduce them to you through this book, a tribute to friendship.

My sister Suzanne is an artist. A few years ago she began to spend winters in Florence to avoid the frigid weather and isolation of her home on Vinalhaven, an island off the coast of Maine. It's a joy having my sister, one of my very best friends, living right around the corner, and she now spends most of the year in Florence. Each morning we meet in Piazza Santo Spirto for a coffee at Caffè Ricchi (page 127), then to shop the market or visit the Innocenti brothers (page 148). She's accompanied me on many of my trips, one of which inspired her to paint the watercolor of Vito Santoro (page 235). I fell in love with her watercolors—and the idea of her watercolors illustrating my (and now her) friends for this book. She did, too. Her spectacular paintings make this book special.

I cook with the greatest products: extra virgin olive oil, Parmigiano-Reggiano, pasta made from heirloom wheat, salt-packed capers, canned tuna in oil, dried and frozen chili peppers, artisan-made *salumi* and cured

Note that all restaurants listed are open for both lunch and dinner unless otherwise indicated. Lunch in Italy is usually seated from 12:30 to 2 (but you don't get up from the table until 3 or 4 . . .) and dinner usually starts seating around 8. However, these hours may vary and it is always best to reserve in advance.

In Italy some phone numbers have 4, 5, 6, 7, or 8 digits after the prefix. These are not typos.

Postal codes come before the name of the town or city. If the address is a major city, it will look like this: 80265 Napoli. If it is a small town, it will include the abbreviation of the province, such as 80064 Sant'Agata sui Due Golfi (NA), a town in the province of Napoli.

If an address has a website and no e-mail address, it means there is an e-mail form on the site itself.

meats. With building blocks like these it's easy to throw a meal together just by adding some super-fresh seasonal produce and organic eggs from the market. Search for the very finest foods and wines you can get your hands on. First-rate extra virgin is essential for Italian cooking; expensive, but you're not going to drink the whole bottle at one meal, and the extra expense is worth it—think of it as effortless Tuscan dressing, because you don't have to spend time and effort to make it. Check out the pantry of my website (www.faithwillinger.com) for information about fine Italian products, or visit www.agferrari.com, www.zingermans.com, and www.gustiamo.com.

If you plan to visit Italy, you can use this book as a guide, and track down many of the people mentioned here, and eat in their restaurants or purchase their products. Tell them I sent you and they'll probably become your friends as well. I've organized my friends and their recipes by three geographical areas, useful for travelers: northern and central regions, from the Alps south to Emilia-Romagna and Le Marche; Tuscany, right outside my front door; and the southern regions and islands of Sicily and Sardinia.

Whether you make a personal pilgrimage or simply enjoy the flavors and experiences I've had by cooking the recipes I've collected from my good friends, I hope you'll enjoy the journey as much as I have.

—F. H. W.

Northern and Central Italy

MY ITALIAN ADVENTURES began in northern and central Italy in the 1970s when I researched the first edition of *Eating in Italy*. I traveled on the sunny side of the Alps bordering France, Switzerland, Austria, and Slovenia, to cities on the Tyrrhenian and Adriatic Seas, through the flatlands of the Po, along the spine of the Apennine Mountains running down the center of the boot. I learned about regional foods and wines from their producers, who turned me onto the cool restaurants. Though sadly the friends and their recipes from Valle d'Aosta, Liguria, Lombardia, and Umbria didn't make the final cut for reasons of space, readers and travelers can meet my friends from Trentino–Alto Adige, Piemonte, Veneto, Friuli–Venezia Giulia, Emilia-Romagna, and Le Marche, and cooks can evoke the experience.

Laura, Nano, Matteo, and Cecilia Morandi

THE VERY BEST CUCINA in Emilia is home cooking, and Laura Morandi prepares phenomenal homestyle cucina at Hosteria Giusti, the restaurant of my dreams. Tucked behind the Giusti grocery on Via Farini, one of the main streets of Modena, Hosteria Giusti is tiny—only five tables. Most diners enter the restaurant through the shop, which is both more fun and far easier than finding the official address of Vicolo Squallore. Laura's husband, Nano, died last year, and his daughter Cecilia now runs the shop, crammed with excellent products like local prosciutto, Parmigiano-Reggiano, bottles of youthful, adolescent and ancient balsamic vinegars displayed in a case, as well as outer-regional items like Carnaroli rice, Sicilian belly tuna, and much, much more. Nano would lead lucky diners to the restaurant through a hallway lined with crates and bottles from impressive wineries, passing the kitchen where Laura would create first-rate traditional Modenese cooking. All pasta is hand-rolled; it's silky and feels different in the mouth from machine-rolled pasta. Carnivores will have a good time, but vegetarians or those on a low-cholesterol diet should probably dine elsewhere.

Meals customarily begin with Gnocco Fritto, a hollow, featherweight pastry pillow paired with Gorgonzola, prosciutto, or, best of all, culatello. Tiny tortellini swimming in capon broth are sublime, worth a voyage, and the deep-fried minestrone fritters are irresistible. Capon salad drizzled with ancient balsamic vinegar is another unbeatable combination. Pork fans will appreciate a wide range of main dishes, including *cotechino in galera* (sausage wrapped in veal and stewed) and braised ribs. I'm not a dessert lover, but Laura's panna cotta, served with the cooked grape must known as *sapa,* is the best I've ever encountered, and her homemade cakes are hard to resist. There's no actual wine list—drink the house Lambrusco or check out the cellar across the alley from the dining

HOSTERIA GIUSTI
Shop: Via Farini, 75
Restaurant: Vicolo Squallore, 46
41100 Modena (MO)
Tel/Fax: +39-059-222-533
Hosteria open for lunch only,
closed Sundays and summer
months; shop closed Thursday
afternoons and Sundays.
All credit cards accepted.

room for something far more important from the well-chosen selection of Italian, French, and even American wines. Hosteria Giusti is open for lunch only (unless you want to reserve the whole restaurant, for eighteen to twenty-six diners) and closed for meals in July and August, when it's too hot to eat this kind of cooking.

Laura's cooking is labor-intensive, requiring skills that can't be duplicated by machine. I'd never attempt most of the dishes she prepares—I can't get the ingredients and haven't got the time or dexterity with a rolling pin to execute them. But her Gnocco Fritto is not too difficult to make and is perfect paired with *salumi* or soft cheese like Gorgonzola or Taleggio. In the States, White Lily makes a soft wheat flour that would be a good stand in for "00" flour; order it at www.whitelily.com.

ANTIPASTO

GNOCCO FRITTO

SERVES 6 TO 8

¼-ounce package (2½ teaspoons) active dry yeast

2 tablespoons warm water (105–115°F.)

2 cups soft wheat flour (Italian "00" or White Lily flour)

1½ teaspoons fine sea salt

2 tablespoons unsalted butter, melted

½ cup club soda or sparkling water

2–3 cups olive oil, for frying

5–6 ounces thinly sliced prosciutto di Parma, or 4–6 ounces
    Gorgonzola or Taleggio, at room temperature

In a small bowl, stir the yeast into the warm water and let stand until foamy, about 5 minutes.

In a large bowl, whisk together the flour and salt. Make a well in the center. Add the melted butter and club soda or sparkling water. Stir mixture until it just forms a dough.

On a lightly floured surface, with floured hands, knead the dough for 1 minute or until it holds together (it will not be smooth). Transfer the dough to a lightly oiled bowl, turning it to coat, and with a sharp knife, cut a shallow *x* on the top. Let the dough rise, loosely covered with a kitchen towel, for 1 hour. (The dough will rise but will not double in bulk.)

Punch down and cut the dough into four pieces. Cover three of them with plastic wrap. On a lightly floured surface, with a floured rolling pin, roll out the fourth piece into a ⅛-inch-thick rectangle (about 12 by 6 inches). With a fluted pastry wheel, cut the dough lengthwise into 2-inch-wide strips, then cut the strips into 2-inch-wide diamonds or squares. Transfer to a dry kitchen towel, arranged in one layer. Make more diamonds or squares with the remaining three pieces of dough in the same manner.

In a 2-quart heavy saucepan, heat the oil over moderate heat until a deep-fat thermometer registers 375°F.

Working in batches of four, fry the diamond/squares, turning them occasionally, until puffed and golden brown, about 2 minutes. With a slotted spoon, transfer them to paper towels or brown paper to drain. Return the oil to 375°F. between batches.

Serve the gnocchi immediately, each topped with a folded slice of prosciutto or a smear of Gorgonzola or Taleggio.

* * *

Josco and Nerina Devetak; Gabriella Cottali

**TRATTORIA
GOSTILNA
DEVETAK**

Via San Michele del Carso, 48
34070 Savogna D'Isonzo (GO)
Tel: +39-0481-882-005
Fax: +39-0481-882-488
info@devetak.com
www.devetak.com
Closed Mondays and Tuesdays;
dinner only on Wednesdays,
Thursdays, and Fridays;
closed 15 days in February
and 15 days in July.
All credit cards accepted.

T HE DEVETAK FAMILY'S eponymous *gostilna* (Slovenian for "trattoria") is in the Carso area of Friuli–Venezia Giulia, outside the city of Gradisca d'Izonso, and has been in operation for more than 100 years. It's difficult to find, located on a narrow road that winds up Monte San Michele, but it came highly recommended by my friend Leda della Rovere (page 38), and I knew it would be worth the trip. Agostino (call him Josco) and his sister Nerina bustle through the two attractive, rustic dining rooms; his wife, Gabriella, prepares exceptional food with herbs and vegetables from their garden. The cucina is based on, but not tied to, regional tradition, and the menu, which changes monthly, is written in Slovenian—and fortunately in Italian, too.

The influences of the Austro-Hungarian Empire are also evident in the presence of spices like nutmeg and cinnamon, and attention to pastry, but mountain flavors like smoky speck and ricotta get their due as well. The pasta is homemade and sauced with mushrooms or game in season; barley is prepared in the manner of risotto, flavored with vegetables and herbs; gnocchi are stuffed with red currants (plums are frequently tucked into gnocchi in Friuli). Braised hare, deer, and grilled boar chops are among the main-course options. Vegetable lovers will appreciate the vegetarian tasting menu. Save room for *ghibaniza* (raisin-studded yeast bread soaked with grappa and sprinkled with sugar), *struklji kuhani* (walnut cookies), mascarpone and coffee custard, or a chocolate and whipped cream confection. Josco is positively obsessed with wine, and we bonded over his well-chosen wine list, which is vast, personal, and a joy to drink from. Among the many bargains on the list are unfamiliar wines made with equally unfamiliar Slovenian grapes, plus wines from the Venezia Giulia region of Friuli and beyond. Dine outside on a deck overlooking the garden when the weather is warm.

Meals often begin with Gabriella's "strudel," a frittata rolled around a filling of goat cheese and arugula, graced with a creamy Tocai sauce. Despite its rich ingredients, the recipe has become a favorite in my home.

FRITTATA DI STRUDEL WITH TOCAI ZABAGLIONE

SERVES 6

1 cup soft, mild goat cheese

1 cup chopped arugula leaves

Salt and freshly ground white pepper

Butter, for preparing the baking pan

6 whole eggs and 3 egg yolks

2⅔ cups heavy cream

⅓ cup Friulian Tocai or other floral white wine

Preheat the oven to 325°F.

Beat the goat cheese and arugula with a mixer, season with salt and pepper, and set aside.

Measure a piece of parchment paper to amply fit a 17½ by 12½-inch jellyroll pan and butter the parchment. Place a tiny smear of butter in the center of the pan and paste the parchment paper onto the pan.

In a large bowl, whisk together the whole eggs, 2 cups of the cream, ½ teaspoon salt, and white pepper until well combined. Pour the mixture into the pan and bake in the middle of the oven until set, about 15 minutes.

While the frittata is baking, prepare the sauce. In the top of a double boiler or a small, deep metal bowl, beat the yolks and the wine until well combined. Set the top of the double boiler or bowl over a saucepan of simmering water and beat with a hand-held electric mixer until tripled in

(recipe continues)

volume—beaters will leave a clear path. Remove top of double boiler or bowl from pan and beat in remaining ⅔ cup cream. Return top or bowl to double boiler or saucepan, whisking constantly, until sauce thickens. Season with salt and pepper. Keep the sauce warm over the double boiler or saucepan, but not on a heat source, while finishing the frittata.

Remove the frittata from the oven and crumble the goat cheese mixture over it, leaving a 1-inch border on all sides. With the long side facing you, and using the parchment paper as a guide, roll up the frittata like a jellyroll. Cut the jellyroll diagonally into six slices and serve each slice with warm sauce.

Andrea and Emanuela Canton, Lidia DeBiasio, Pierangelo Dalmas

I MET ANDREA (in Italy it's a guy's name) Canton in the kitchen of Villa Mozart, a now-defunct Michelin-starred inn in the village of Merano, where he'd come to study with owner/master chef Andreas Hellrigl. The son of restaurateurs in Friuli, Andrea was to participate in a young chef's competition in France and had been sent to spend time in Hellrigl's kitchen for some finishing touches.

LA PRIMULA
Via San Rocco, 47
33080 San Quirino (PN)
Tel: +39-0434-910-05
Fax: +39-0434-917-563
info@ristorantelaprimula.it
www.ristorantelaprimula.it
Closed January 1 to 15, July 10 to 31. Open Tuesday–Saturday, closed Sunday evening and all day Monday.

I, too, was in the kitchen to learn from the maestro, and Andrea and I bonded over kitchen chores, scooping zucchini into pea-size balls, "turning" potatoes and carrots into tiny footballs. We also learned about quality ingredients, tasted our first *balsamico,* made risotto with Vialone Nano rice. We observed as Hellrigl killed and boned a still-moving eel, spread it with black truffle purée, rolled it up, and placed it in a baking dish— watching it twitch on its way to the oven. When Andrea placed third in the competition, behind French and Swiss chefs, I had to visit the family restaurant to congratulate him.

Ristorante La Primula, in the Piemontese village of San Quirino, outside the provincial capital of Pordenone, began as a family trattoria, with guestrooms upstairs where hunters used to spend the night. Andreas Hellrigl's culinary lessons influenced Andrea when he joined his mother, Lidia DeBiasio, in the kitchen (known for its homemade bread and preserves and obsessively superior ingredients), and the cucina at La Primula became more sophisticated, open to products from other Italian regions. Andrea's sister Emanuela and her husband, sommelier Pierangelo Dalmus, who's crazy about Friuli's fine wines, have now replaced Andrea's father and brother in the dining room.

Andrea's squash soufflé is typical of his cucina—not traditional, but utilizing fine local ingredients like winter squash, ricotta, pancetta, and aged Montasio. If you can't find Montasio, use Parmigiano-Reggiano. Vegetarians can easily eliminate the pork.

ANTIPASTO

WINTER SQUASH AND CHEESE SOUFFLÉ WITH SQUASH SAUCE
(AND CRISPY PANCETTA, IF YOU LIKE)

SERVES 6

SAUCE

½ pound winter squash, peeled and cubed (1 cup)

Sea salt

1 tablespoon butter or extra virgin olive oil

Freshly ground black pepper

SOUFFLÉ

About 1 pound butternut squash, halved and seeds removed

16 thin slices smoked pancetta or bacon

½ cup ricotta

6 tablespoons butter, at room temperature, plus more for buttering
    the molds

2 tablespoons cornmeal, for dusting

¾ cup grated aged Montasio cheese or
    Parmigiano-Reggiano cheese

3 eggs, at room temperature

Sea salt and freshly ground pepper

⅓ cup soft wheat flour (Italian "00" or White Lily flour)

Freshly ground black pepper

Make the sauce first. Simmer the squash in 1½ cups water and 2 teaspoons salt until tender, 20 to 30 minutes. Drain the squash, reserving the liquid. Purée the squash, and then add some of the cooking water to make a sauce slightly thicker than heavy cream. Heat 1 tablespoon butter or extra virgin in a small saucepan, add the squash purée, season with salt and pepper, and simmer for a minute or two. Set aside.

Preheat the oven to 375°F.

Make the soufflés. Bake the squash cut side down for about 1 hour, until tender when pierced with a fork. Meanwhile, bake 12 slices of pancetta or bacon in the oven for 20 to 25 minutes, until crisp and browned. Drain on paper towels.

Cool the squash, scoop out the flesh, and measure ½ cup. Purée the squash with the ricotta.

Generously butter six ½-cup molds and dust with cornmeal.

Beat the butter and the cheese until well mixed and pale. Add the eggs, one at a time, beating well after each addition. Add the squash-ricotta mixture, then add salt and pepper to taste. Fold in the flour. Divide mixture among the molds and bake for 12 to 15 minutes, until lightly browned and puffed.

While soufflés are baking, cut the remaining slices of pancetta or bacon into thin strips and sauté over medium heat until crisp. Drain on a paper towel.

When soufflés are done, spoon some of the warm squash sauce on six individual serving dishes, unmold the soufflés onto the plates, each flanked by two pancetta or bacon slices. Scatter the pancetta or bacon strips on the soufflés.

* * *

Claudia and Tonino Verro

M Y VERY FIRST TRIP to Piemonte brought me to La Contea, the restaurant of Claudia and Tonino Verro in the adorable hilltop village of Neive. Claudia cooked while Tonino worked the front of the house, and I was impressed with their combination of rustic food and an elegant county-style setting. I returned to stay in the somewhat shabby but very convenient rooms upstairs, sitting in the kitchen talking to Claudia, haunting the regional truffle markets at dawn with Tonino, drinking Barbaresco and Barbera with both of them until 3 A.M.—and watching them build an empire in Neive.

They have since upgraded their rooms and added a few more next door to their home and have also built a small winery, all while dishing out the same regional food that made me fall in love with La Contea. The dining rooms are formal without being stuffy, lit by candlelight in the evening with fireplaces glowing in the winter. Tonino Verro guides diners through Claudia's menu and his glorious wine list of regional gems served in appropriately large crystal glasses. Tonino's truffle-market excursions in the late fall and early winter supply the restaurant with fantastic white truffles, sliced with abandon over many dishes, but even when they're not in season the cucina doesn't disappoint. Claudia serves *tartra* with different seasonal toppings—white truffles in preserved black truffles, sautéed porcini mushrooms, or asparagus—but says not to even think about using truffle oil, a totally artificial product that has no place in the kitchen.

LA CONTEA

Piazza Cocito, 8
12057 Neive (CN)
Tel: +39-0173-671-26
or +39-0173-677-558
Fax: +39-0173-673-67
lacontea@la-contea.it
www.la-contea.it
Open every day September–
November; closed February 1–mid-
March. Closed Sunday evenings
and all Monday, March–August.
All credit cards accepted.

FLAN WITH MUSHROOMS, ASPARAGUS, OR TRUFFLES

SERVES 6

1 medium onion, chopped

1 tablespoon butter

1 teaspoon fresh sage leaves

1 teaspoon fresh rosemary leaves

2 cups heavy cream

½ cup whole milk

4 eggs

⅓ cup grated Parmigiano-Reggiano cheese

Salt and freshly ground black pepper to taste

Grating of nutmeg

Extra virgin olive oil, to coat the baking dishes

½ pound mushrooms or asparagus (or fresh white or black truffles, if you should be so lucky)

1 tablespoon unsalted butter (if topping with mushrooms or asparagus)

1 garlic clove, chopped (if topping with mushrooms or asparagus)

Preheat the oven to 325°F.

Sauté the onion in 1 tablespoon butter over low heat until soft. Add the herbs and purée the mixture in a blender or food processor.

In a bowl, mix the cream, milk, eggs, Parmigiano, salt and pepper, and nutmeg. Add the onion and herb purée.

Brush six ½-cup baking dishes with extra virgin and fill with the egg mixture. Set the dishes in a pan of hot water (bain marie) and bake for 50 minutes or until the custards are set.

While they bake, clean and slice the mushrooms or asparagus, or carefully clean your truffles. Unless you are using truffles, heat 1 tablespoon of the butter and add the garlic. Add the mushrooms or asparagus, and sauté until tender. Season with salt and pepper

Serve each flan with a spoonful of sautéed mushrooms or asparagus on the side, or top with thinly shaved truffles.

Thomas Rossi

I MET THOMAS ROSSI at VinItaly, the annual wine fair. Our friend Ivan Bertelli had hired him to work at the Cavicchioli stand, and they were serving Lambrusco along with snacks like mortadella, culatello, super-fresh raw langoustines, and oysters. The stand was packed, amazing, since fair attendees can taste important (and expensive) wines such as Barolo, Barbaresco, and Brunello at hundreds of stands. My next

OH, PERBACCO!
Via XXIV Maggio, 5
42048 Rubiera (RE)
Tel: +39-0522-626-643
ohperbacco@tin.it
www.ohperbacco.it
Open in the evenings only;
closed Tuesdays.

encounter was at Ivan's restaurant, where Thomas entered one night through a window to join me and a group of American friends halfway through dinner. Watching him slash the tops off Champagne bottles with a serving spoon and slice salami for a snack after dinner made me eager to visit his enoteca in Rubiera, population 6,000.

Thomas's enoteca is called Oh, Perbacco, a reference to Bacchus but also an Italian golly-gee-whiz expression that doesn't begin to communicate my (and everyone else's) reaction to this very special wine bar. Thomas approaches the wine business like a warrior, selling more than 3,500 bottles of Champagne yearly. The enoteca is patronized by local kids, workers in overalls just out of the factory, businesspeople in suits and loosened ties, and stylish Italian women in stiletto heels—all drinking Champagne—and the atmosphere is always festive. When Thomas asks customers what kind of wine they love, he always recommends something much better that is less expensive, and in the process earns their undying loyalty. The snacks at Oh, Perbacco are fantastic, and the little meatballs are different from any others I've tasted. Vegetarians can leave out the meatballs and enjoy the salad with just the fried onions and balsamic dressing.

ANTIPASTO

LITTLE MEATBALL SALAD
(AND A VEGETARIAN POSSIBILITY)

SERVES 6 TO 8

½ pound yellow-fleshed potatoes, such as Yukon Gold
10 ounces lean ground meat, either 7 ounces pork and 3 ounces
   beef or all beef
2 cups grated Parmigiano-Reggiano cheese
2 tablespoons minced fresh parsley

1 small garlic clove, minced

3 eggs

Salt and freshly ground black pepper

⅓ cup fine bread crumbs

½–¾ cup plus 1 tablespoon extra virgin olive oil

¼ cup flour

1 onion, thinly sliced

1½–2 cups vegetable oil

4 cups mâche or small, tender salad greens

Aged balsamico, or 1 cup conventional balsamic boiled with

    2 tablespoons sugar until syrupy and reduced by one-third

Boil the potatoes until tender, drain, then peel and mash. Add them to the meat with the Parmigiano, parsley, garlic, and eggs. Season with salt and pepper and form the mixture into meatballs the size of a small walnut. Put the bread crumbs in a paper bag and add the meatballs, six or eight at a time, and shake them in the bag to coat with crumbs. Repeat with remaining meatballs.

Heat ¼ cup extra virgin in a skillet until hot, and working in batches, sauté the meatballs in a single layer until browned all over. Repeat until all the meatballs are cooked. Drain on paper towels.

Put the flour in a paper bag. Divide the onion slices into rings, and rinse them with water. Drain well and shake off excess water, but don't dry. Put the onion rings in the bag, then shake the bag to coat the rings lightly with flour.

Heat the vegetable oil to 375°F in a small pot. Deep-fry the onion rings until crisp. Drain on paper towels.

Put the mâche or salad greens on a serving platter, dress with 1 tablespoon extra virgin and salt and pepper. Top the salad with the meatballs and the onion rings. Drizzle with balsamic vinegar.

Ferretti Family: Silvana, Armando, Walter, Giuseppina, Roberto, Patrizia, and Alice

IL CASCINALE NUOVO

Statale Asti-Alba, 15

14057 Isola d'Asti (AT)

Tel: +39-0141-958-166

Fax: +39-0141-958-828

info@ilcascinalenuovo.it

www.ilcascinalenuovo.it

Dinner only except Sundays;

closed Sunday evenings

and all day Monday.

Closed 15 days in August

and 15 days in January.

All credit cards accepted.

I MET THE FERRETTI BROTHERS, Roberto (dining room, sommelier) and Walter (chef), at their restaurant/inn, Il Cascinale Nuovo, which I use as a base for touring Piemonte. It's conveniently located near a main highway, and has a swimming pool to cool off when it's hot, modern rooms, and a few suites, all well priced. On my first visit, I found the whole family hard at work. The Ferrettis' mother, Silvana, and grandmother Giuseppina were tending a huge black cauldron in the backyard, putting up tomato sauce for the winter while Silvana's husband, Armando, after delivering a supply of tomatoes to the women, made a breakfast of homemade preserves, fruit juice, cake, and perfect cappuccino for the guests. When I expressed my interest, Armando took me to the fruit and vegetable market the next morning. I went down the back stairs to the kitchen to see what Walter was preparing. I discussed winery visits with Roberto and his wife, Patrizia. After a few days I felt like a member of the family, as do most guests at Il Cascinale Nuovo.

The restaurant is modern but not stark, and comfortable, the tables set with important wine glasses. Come prepared to drink some of the finest wines in the region, knowing that driving to a hotel will not be necessary. Walter's menu utilizes traditional, seasonal ingredients in creative preparations that are beautifully presented. More attention is paid to dining in this area during white truffle season, but Walter's cooking is worth a voyage year-round, and since Roberto's daughter Alice has joined him in the dining room, the service is better than ever.

Walter's tartlet recipe tucks white truffles between the squash and Parmigiano layers, but as I rarely have white truffles I often make this recipe without them or substitute sautéed minced mushrooms. If you are fortunate enough to have a fresh white truffle, do slip a slice or two between the layers, then garnish each serving with extra truffle. The cheese is easiest to slice off a larger chunk.

WINTER SQUASH AND PARMIGIANO TARTLETS

SERVES 4

FILLING

6 ounces fresh mushrooms (chanterelles or porcini,
    cremini as a last choice; optional)
¼ cup extra virgin olive oil, plus 2 tablespoons if using mushrooms
Salt and freshly ground black pepper
1 butternut squash or any other firm-fleshed winter squash that can
    be sliced, peeled (should weigh 1 pound after peeling)
3-ounce piece of Parmigiano-Reggiano cheese, sliced ⅛ inch thick
    with a mandoline

SAUCE

¾ cup heavy cream
½ cup grated Parmigiano-Reggiano cheese
1 tablespoon butter
Fine salt and freshly ground white pepper
Small grating of nutmeg

Make the filling. If using the mushrooms, clean and mince; if using porcini or chanterelles, mince the stems and thinly slice the caps. Heat 2 tablespoons of the extra virgin in a nonstick pan, add the mushrooms, and sauté over high heat until mushrooms are lightly browned or mushroom water has evaporated. This mixure should be dry. Season with salt and pepper and set aside.

(recipe continues)

Cut the squash into ¼-inch slices with a mandoline or sharp knife. Heat 1 tablespoon of the extra virgin in a large nonstick skillet and sauté a layer of squash slices over medium heat until lightly browned. Turn the slices over and cook the other side. Remove. Cook the remaining squash, a layer at a time, adding a tablespoon of extra virgin for each batch. Drain the slices on paper towels, then season lightly with salt and pepper.

Preheat the oven to 375°F.

Line the bottom and sides of four ⅔-cup ramekins or metal molds with the squash slices. Top the squash with a layer of Parmigiano slices. Add 1 teaspoon of the mushroom mixture if using. Continue layering cheese and squash (but not mushrooms) until all the squash is used or the molds are full. (If there's any extra cheese it can be used in the sauce.)

Bake the molds for 10 to 15 minutes. While they bake, prepare the sauce.

Heat the cream until hot, add the grated Parmigiano, stir to combine well, then whisk in the butter. Season with salt, pepper, and nutmeg. Keep the sauce warm.

Unmold the squash cups onto individual plates, surround with sauce, and garnish with remaining mushroom mixture.

Massimiliano, Raffaele, Rita, Erminio, and Laura Alajmo

I WAS FIRST INVITED to Le Calandre to speak at a winemaker dinner. At this restaurant located outside Padova, not far from Venice, Raffaele Alajmo was in charge of the dining room with his father Erminio, while younger brother Massimiliano and mother Rita were in the kitchen. The dinner was successful, and afterward the brothers sabered open bottles of Champagne, a bonding experience. The next day Massi took me shopping, Rita invited me into the pastry kitchen, and Raf showed me the wine cellar. I also had a chance to check out the bar in front of the restaurant, managed by sister Laura, who is clearly as obsessed with quality as everyone else in the family. She offered special roast coffee, homemade chocolates, and some of the best pastries I've ever tasted—some made with natural yeast starter that's more than twenty years old.

Over the years Le Calandre has earned three Michelin stars and the highest ratings from Italian guidebooks. Rita and Erminio run a restaurant at the nearby Montecchia Golf Club and the family took over the nondescript hotel next to their restaurant, transforming it into the Maccaroni Hotel, with fantastic amenities and bent forks to hold the room keys. Massi and Raf opened Il Calandrino, a casual restaurant next to the bar that serves breakfast, lunch, dinner, and snacks from 8 A.M. to midnight with an open kitchen so customers can watch the action. For a perfect culinary souvenir, visit the Alajmos' gourmet grocery right across the street, named for their gourmand grandfather Vittorio, which carries exceptional products from Italy and beyond, and even a fantastic take-out menu.

Massi and Raf wrote an interesting cookbook, *in.gredienti,* which they begged me to translate. I did, with Jenn, just to learn their secrets, and it was the most difficult job of my life. Most recipes were ultra-complicated,

RISTORANTE LE CALANDRE AND HOTEL MACCARONI

Via Liguria, 1
35030 Sarmeola di Rubano (PD)
Tel: +39-049-630-303
Fax: +39-049-633-000
alajmo@calandre.com
www.calandre.com
Closed Sundays and Mondays;
closed December 25–January 20
and August 6–30.

VERANDA IL CALANDRINO

Contacts are the same as above
Closed Mondays; open all year
8 A.M. to midnight.

composed of eight or more elements and requiring tools like a chill blaster and vacuum-packer. I was inspired to make up my own recipe, using part of one dish (eggplant) with two elements from another (ricotta cream and tomato tartar). It's a wonderful, easy appetizer and, most important, Massi approves.

<table>
<tr><td>ANTIPASTO</td><td>

EGGPLANT PURÉE WITH RICOTTA CREAM AND TOMATO TARTAR

</td></tr>
</table>

EGGPLANT PURÉE

1 eggplant, preferably violet, ¾ pound

3 or 4 spearmint leaves

½ teaspoon salt

¼ teaspoon sugar

Drop of traditional balsamic vinegar

1–2 tablespoons extra virgin olive oil

Drop of garlic oil

RED TOMATO TARTAR

1 pound vine-ripened tomatoes

½ pound cherry tomatoes

1 teaspoon fine sea salt

½ teaspoon sugar

1 tablespoon extra virgin olive oil

Pinch of ground black pepper

RICOTTA CREAM

4 ounces ricotta (Massimiliano uses buffalo ricotta)

Pinch of sea salt

¼ teaspoon sugar

1 tablespoon extra virgin olive oil

Cut the eggplant in half and make a few lengthwise incisions in the flesh. Place the eggplant in a microwave-safe bowl, cover with plastic wrap, and microwave on high for 10 minutes. When cool enough to handle, remove the skin, discard any excess liquid, and place the flesh in a blender with the remaining eggplant purée ingredients. Puree to make a soft cream. (Alternatively you can use an immersion mixer to blend the eggplant purée ingredients.)

To make the tartar, bring a large pot of water to a boil. Slip the tomatoes and cherry tomatoes into the boiling water for around 10 seconds, remove to a colander, and, when cool enough to handle, peel them and gently squeeze out most of the seeds. Roughly chop the tomatoes in a food processor. Place a sieve with large holes over a bowl, transfer the chopped tomatoes to the sieve, and sprinkle with the salt and sugar. When the liquid has drained from the tomatoes, transfer the pulp to a bowl, reserving the tomato water. Stir the extra virgin into the pulp and season with pepper.

To make the ricotta cream, combine the ricotta, 2 tablespoons of the reserved tomato water, the salt, sugar, and extra virgin in a blender and purée, or mix with an immersion mixer until creamy.

Put a fourth of the eggplant purée on a plate. Top with a fourth of the ricotta cream and flank with 2 or 3 spoonfuls of tomato tartar. (Form the pulp into quenelles with 2 soup spoons if you want to be fancy; otherwise you can simply spoon it directly onto the serving dishes.) Garnish, of course, with a drizzle of extra virgin.

Massimo and Lara Bottura

OSTERIA FRANCESCANA

Via Stella, 22

41100 Modena

Tel: +39-059 210-118

Fax: +39-059 220-286

Closed Saturdays at lunch and all day Sunday; closed in August and December 23–January 12.

All credit cards accepted.

ENOTECA LA FRANCESCHETTA

Via Vignolese, 58

41100 Modena

Tel: +39-059-309-1008

ALTHOUGH I WAS RELUCTANT to visit Osteria Francescana at first (I'd been told by a friend that they had *piatti americani,* only to find that the dishes were imported from Fishs Eddy in America), once I did go it was easy to fall in love. The restaurant was a jewel, with beautiful modern paintings on the walls; a menu based on regional, seasonal ingredients; a fantastic wine list; and a chef totally committed to a new, lighter way of cooking. Alain Ducasse had dined at Osteria Francescana in the early '90s and invited chef-owner Massimo Bottura to spend time in his kitchen. Massimo returned with new ideas, which he applied to local ingredients and dishes, steaming cotecchino sausage over Lambrusco instead of boiling it in water, creating a creamy sauce of broth and Parmigiano instead of butter and cream, becoming a fervent believer in extra virgin olive oil. Then, in 1999, Ferran Adrià dined at the osteria and invited Massimo to spend two months in the kitchen at El Bulli. Once again, he returned home with lots to think about.

In addition to the stimulation of Ducasse and Adrià, Massimo credits his wife Lara (a modern art curator) with helping him understand the structure of cuisine, drawing on the concepts and language of art. He has looked for food artisans who were dreamers, who made special products. He has experimented with gelatins and foams, textures, three different ages of Parmigiano-Reggiano, ethereal rabbit covered with a thin gelatinous veil of balsamic vinegar. But he has never entirely turned his back on tradition, retaining a *sfoglina* pasta roller to come in each day to make fresh pasta; hand-formed tortellini in capon broth is always on the menu for traditionalists. They're the kinds of dishes that are a pleasure to look at and taste, but not easily re-created in the home kitchen. So instead I'm sharing one of Massimo's recipes that uses his fine Villa Manodori balsamic vinegar, classically paired with potatoes and onions in a delicate soup. Massimo has just opened Enoteca Franceschetta, where wine is sold by the bottle and glass, along with fine *salumi,* cheese, and some of Osteria Francescana's creative appetizers.

OLD-STYLE WHITE ONION SOUP

SERVES 6

1 pound white onions
8 shallots
1 tablespoon extra virgin olive oil
¾ pound potatoes (russet or baking potatoes)
5 cups capon or chicken broth
Sea salt and freshly ground black pepper
Extra virgin olive oil and 25-year-old balsamic vinegar, for serving

Slice the onions and shallots, drizzle with the 1 tablespoon extra virgin, and cook over the lowest heat in a heavy-bottomed casserole (Massimo says in a heavy copper pot) for 40 minutes.

While the onions are cooking, peel the potatoes, cut into 1-inch chunks, and steam over boiling water for 10 minutes.

Add the potatoes to the cooked onions, add the broth, and simmer until the potatoes are very tender.

Purée the soup with a food mill or immersion blender. Taste for salt and pepper. Drizzle each portion of soup with 1 teaspoon extra virgin and ½ teaspoon balsamic vinegar.

* * *

Leda della Rovere; Livio, Maurizio, Elda, and Andrea Felluga

OSTERIA TERRA & VINI

Via XXIV Maggio

34071 Brazzano di Cormons (GO)

Tel: +39-0481-600-26

Fax: +39-0481-639-198

info@terraevini.it

www.terraevini.it

Closed Wednesdays.

All credit cards accepted.

I WAS INVITED to the Livio Felluga winery to attend a dinner for a group of visiting wine reps in the *foresteria* (guesthouse), and though I enjoyed meeting Livio and his children Maurizio, Elda, and Andrea, and I was impressed with the wines, I spent more time in the kitchen than at the table. The woman responsible for the wonderful food, Leda della Rovere, made me promise a return trip to nearby Manzano, where her mother Romea had an eponymous bar-restaurant.

Manzano is the world's chair capital, a distinction attested to by the 20-meter-tall red fir chair monument on route SS56. It's way too big for anyone to sit in, but definitely a photo op and a cultural excuse to visit. Da Romea was nearby. The bar was typical of Friuli, with tables of card-playing, smoking, drinking men reading the pink and black *Gazzetta dello Sport,* betting on the results of soccer matches, and buying lottery tickets. The restaurant, with a large *fogolar* onion-domed fireplace in the center, was off to one side. I'd visit whenever I went to Friuli–Venezia Giulia, thrilled by the warmth of their enthusiastic greeting in dialect, *"Mandi,"* Leda's homestyle cooking, and her brother Gianni's grilling at the *fogolar.* I viewed with dismay the renovations made by an overenthusiastic architect, including the inappropriate stained-glass door that separated bar from restaurant. When Gianni died the restaurant was closed, but Leda is back with the Felluga family, cooking at Terra & Vini, Osteria con Alloggio, their eight-room inn next to the winery. The short menu is written on a blackboard and features four daily specials, first-rate prosciutto, *salumi* and cheese, and a selection of Felluga wines by the bottle or glass.

Leda's recipe for barley "risotto" is easier to execute than risotto and will hold without getting gummy. Vegetarians can leave out the sausage and add more butter (or extra virgin), and even change the recipe as Leda does, using her favorite seasonal vegetables like zucchini, winter squash, wild greens (or spinach, if you can't find anything wild), red radicchio, or mushrooms instead of leeks.

LEEK AND SAUSAGE ORZOTTO

SERVES 4 TO 6

1 cup pearl barley
4 leeks
Sea salt
6–8 ounces fresh sausage
¼ cup unsalted butter (or extra virgin, if you're like me)
2 tablespoons dry white wine
½ cup freshly grated Parmigiano-Reggiano cheese
2 teaspoons minced fresh parsley
Freshly ground black pepper

In a bowl, cover the barley with about 4 cups of cold water and soak for 3 to 6 hours. Drain in a colander.

Clean the leeks, saving the tough ends and outer leaves for the vegetable stock. Chop the tender parts of the leeks. Combine the leek trimmings with 8 cups water and 2 tablespoons sea salt, and simmer for 30 to 45 minutes.

Sauté the sausage in a nonstick skillet, breaking it up, until it loses its pink color and renders its fat. Drain the fat and reserve the sausage.

In a 5-quart saucepan, sauté the chopped leeks with 2 tablespoons butter or extra virgin over low heat until wilted. Add the white wine, raise the heat to evaporate the wine, then add the barley and 2 cups simmering broth. Cook over moderate heat, stirring frequently, until thickened and

(recipe continues)

most broth has been absorbed. Add more simmering broth, 1 cup at a time, until the broth is absorbed. When barley is almost done, in around 10 minutes, add the drained sausage and begin adding broth ½ cup at a time. Cook until the barley is tender, probably an additional 10 minutes. You may not need all the broth. Stir in the Parmigiano-Reggiano, the remaining 2 tablespoons butter (or extra virgin), the parsley, and pepper until well mixed, and remove from heat. Barley should be slightly soupy, a consistency that will slip across a plate. Let the orzotto stand for 5 minutes before serving.

Ampelio Bucci and Vanda Bernasconi

AMPELIO. Based on the Greek word *ampelios,* "grape vine" or "vineyard," it's a most unusual name for a most unusual winery owner. We first met at VinItaly, the annual Italian wine fair, where I was attracted to the classy modern stand (cool displays, lamps, chairs, no wine barrels) that he shared with designers Afra and Tobia Scarpa. (They had the same consulting enologist for their winery in Veneto.) Ampelio Bucci has a day job as a marketing consultant in Milan, but when he inherited a family farm in Le Marche in the late 1970s, he hired a skillful winemaker to make traditional wines: Verdicchio and Rosso Piceno. No New Wave chardonnay, cabernet, merlot, or syrah, no barriques. The region had previously been known more for the quantity than the quality of its wines, Verdicchio's amphora-shaped bottles its only distinction. Villa Bucci's wines started an enological revolution, and the area's fine restaurants responded with enthusiasm. Reserve Verdicchio Villa Bucci is my favorite Italian white wine, and it resembles its producer—elegant, singular, better with age.

I visited Ampelio and met Vanda, his stylish wife, buyer for Neiman Marcus, at his ancestral home in Montecarotto. Although dinner was served in the formal dining room of their art deco villa, it began with a rustic dish—polenta served on a wooden board topped with tomato sauce and cheese, half sprinkled with sausage—which diners scooped directly onto their plates. Ampelio explained that those with fewer financial resources would make a simple tomato sauce and place a single sausage in the center of the polenta, a reward for the fastest eater.

AZIENDA AGRICOLA F.LLI BUCCI
Via Cona, 30
60010 Ostra Vetere (AN)
Tel/Fax: +39-071-964-179
bucciwines@villabucci.com
www.villabucci.com
Visits by appointment only.

POLENTA WITH TOMATO SAUCE AND SAUSAGE RAGÙ

FIRST COURSE

SERVES 6 TO 8

1 cup cornmeal for polenta

Sea salt

2 garlic cloves

2 tablespoons extra virgin olive oil

2 cups diced canned or fresh tomatoes

Freshly ground black pepper

4 Italian sausages (or 1 large sausage for the rustic version)

½ cup grated Parmigiano-Reggiano cheese

Bring 6 cups of water to a boil in a 3-quart pot. Slowly sprinkle the cornmeal into the water, stirring with a whisk to prevent lumping. Add 1 teaspoon sea salt. Place the pot in another, larger pot of boiling water or a double boiler, and cook over low heat for 45 minutes or until creamy, not too thick.

Sauté the garlic in the extra virgin until it begins to color. Add the

(recipe continues)

tomatoes and cook over medium heat for around 5 minutes, or until they look softened. Season with salt and pepper.

Remove the casings from the sausages and crumble into a nonstick pan. Sauté over medium-high heat until lightly brown, smashing with a wooden fork to break up sausage. There should be enough fat in the meat to brown the sausage; if there's a lot of water, cook to evaporate it. Drain the sausage meat and set aside.

Pour the polenta onto a clean cutting board and spread into a layer around 1½ inches thick. Spread the tomato sauce over the polenta. Scatter the sausage meat over half the polenta and sprinkle with Parmigiano-Reggiano. (Or sprinkle with Parmigiano and place the single sausage in the center of the polenta.) Serve immediately.

Carla, Carlo, Michele, and Teresa Latini

IT FEELS LIKE I've known Carla and Carlo Latini forever. I was introduced to their first-rate pasta at Cesare Benelli's restaurant in Venice, and I was an instant convert. Their phone number was on the pasta box, so I called to order a few cases. They came to visit me in Florence, and we bonded over a plate of spaghetti. I visited them in turn in Le Marche, where a legendary agronomist-consultant pointed out the heirloom varietals, with their inherent advantages and defects, that grew in their experimental wheat fields.

Latini pasta is made exclusively from wheat grown in Le Marche, including Senatore Capelli, an heirloom Italian wheat, and Taganrog, the legendary red wheat from Russia. Both of these rare cultivars are harder and higher in protein than most other wheats and so are used to make single-cultivar pastas.

Special bronze dies are used to extrude the Latini pasta, which is then dried slowly—all the right moves to ensure a superior artisanal pasta. The difference between Latini and commercial pasta, extruded from Teflon dies, is easy to see: the surface of Latini's pasta looks sand-blasted, feels rough, and holds on to sauce better. When I cook their pasta, I can smell the difference—it gives off a sweet, wheaty, starchy scent. The extra protein helps the Senatore Capelli and Taganrog pasta remain more resistant to the tooth when cooked. I usually despise emmer (farro) pasta—it's too pasty when cooked—but Latini's is superb in both short shapes like penne and strands like spaghetti.

Carla Latini and I travel in the same circles. Wherever we are—Milan for a chefs' conclave, Verona at VinItaly, Rome for Antonello Colonna's (page 165) book presentation—we often stay at the same hotel and always meet for breakfast. We speak all the time and exchange restaurant news. This recipe, her son Michele's favorite, is made with Latini's Taganrog trenette (another name for linguine) and is sauced with shrimp, potatoes, vegetables, and extra virgin. Use the best pasta you can get your hands on.

PASTIFICIO AZIENDA AGRARIA LATINI S.R.L.
Via Maestri del Lavoro, 19
60027 Osimo (AN)
Tel: +39-071-781-9768
Fax: +39-071-721-1049
info@latini.com
www.latini.com
Visits by appointment only.

TRENETTE WITH POTATOES, SEASONAL VEGETABLES, AND SHRIMP

SERVES 4 TO 6

2 medium potatoes

2 medium zucchini (or green beans or broccoli, or any seasonal
    green vegetable)

3 tablespoons sea salt

14–16 ounces trenette (or spaghetti)

2 garlic cloves, peeled

¼ cup extra virgin olive oil

12–18 medium shrimp, peeled and deveined

2–3 tablespoons chopped fresh basil

Using a mandoline (or knife skills if you're able), cut the potatoes into julienne, for around 1½ cups. Cut the zucchini with the same blade to make around 1½ cups zucchini julienne. (Or cut the green beans or broccoli or other green vegetable into 3 cups of small pieces or strips.)

Bring 5 quarts of water to a rolling boil in a large pot. Add the sea salt and cook the potatoes until tender. Remove from the water with a slotted spoon and set aside in a bowl. Cook the zucchini (or other vegetable) until tender, remove with a slotted spoon, place in a colander, and run cold water over the vegetables (or place in a sinkful of cold water) to cool them. Drain vegetables and add to the potatoes.

Add the pasta to the vegetable cooking water. While the pasta is cooking, put the garlic in a large skillet, drizzle with 1 tablespoon extra virgin, and cook over high heat until the garlic begins to color. Add the shrimp and sauté until they lose their raw look, a minute or two. If shrimp are already cooked, sauté just to heat. Add the cooked vegetables to the pan and turn off the heat.

Cook the pasta until it offers considerable resistance to the tooth, a few minutes from al dente. Drain the pasta, reserving 2 cups of the cooking water. Add the pasta to the vegetables in the skillet along with ½ cup cooking water and cook over high heat for 3 to 5 minutes to complete the cooking, adding more pasta water if sauce dries too much. When the pasta is cooked, add the basil and remaining 3 tablespoons extra virgin.

Gigi Vianello and Momi di Momi

CESARE BENELLI (page 77) told me about Mascaron, owned by his best friend, Gigi Vianello, and Momi di Momi. It started life as a Venetian osteria, a place to snag some *cicchetti* (snacks) and an *ombra* (a glass of wine), but it's evolved into a full-fledged restaurant with wine by the bottle, an extensive menu, and three cozy dining rooms. It has even spawned a wine bar, Mascareta, run by everyone's friend Mauro Lorenzon (page 57) and open evenings only. Mascaron hasn't evolved too far; there are still butcher-paper placemats and wine-colored paper napkins, the menu is hand-written, and you can still get a glass of wine at the bar in between meals. It's one of my favorite places to eat in Venice—fun and filled with Venetians.

Gigi, Cesare, and Momi once met me in Friuli to taste wines and rare cheeses and to visit an artisanal salami-maker. When we got back to Venice, late and hungry, we couldn't find a decent restaurant open. Gigi opened the kitchen at Mascaron, checked out the refrigerator, and whipped up a plate of spaghettini (it cooks faster than spaghetti) with swordfish. It's become a favorite, even when I'm not in a hurry.

OSTERIA AL MASCARON
Castello 5225
Calle Lunga Santa Maria Formosa
30100 Venezia
Tel: +39-041-522-5995
Closed Sundays.

SPAGHETTINI WITH SWORDFISH RAGÙ

SERVES 4 TO 6

8–10 ounces swordfish

2 garlic cloves, chopped

3–4 tablespoons extra virgin olive oil

¼ cup dry white wine

2 cups tomato pulp (peeled and seeded fresh tomatoes)

½ teaspoon minced fresh thyme

Sea salt and freshly ground black pepper

1 tablespoon chopped fresh basil

14–16 ounces spaghettini

Trim the swordfish, eliminating bones and skin, and cut into ¼-inch cubes.

Put the chopped garlic in a large skillet, add the extra virgin, and cook over medium heat until the garlic barely begins to color. Add the swordfish cubes and cook for a few minutes, until they lose their raw look. Add the wine, raise the heat to evaporate most of the wine, then add the tomato pulp, thyme, and salt and pepper. Simmer for 10 minutes, then add the basil.

In a large pot, bring 5 or 6 quarts of water to a rolling boil. Add 2 to 3 tablespoons salt and the spaghettini and cook until the pasta still offers considerable resistance to the tooth, about three-fourths of the package cooking time.

Drain the pasta, reserving 1 cup of the pasta-cooking water. Add the pasta to the sauce in the skillet and, over high heat, cook the pasta together with the sauce to complete the cooking; add some of the reserved pasta water if the sauce dries too much. Serve immediately.

Marie and Brandino Brandolini

BRANDINO AND MARIE BRANDOLINI are beautiful, talented, and fun. As befits their noble heritage (they are, in fact, a count and countess), they live in a palace in Venice and also maintain a villa on the border of Veneto and Friuli. But they're dynamic—he is a vintner, and she works with glassblowers on the island of Murano, with whom she has created a line of glassware and accessories, Laguna B. The lively, modern, brightly colored tumblers, bowls, plates, vases, paperweights, and necklaces follow the rustic Venetian tradition of using leftover bits and pieces of *murrine* beads and rods. In 1980, Brandino, who has a degree in agriculture from Texas A&M, replanted the vineyards of Vistorta, the family estate, using grafts of merlot from relatives at Chateau Greysac in Bordeaux; a consulting French enologist found the terroir of Vistorta ideal for merlot.

LAGUNA B.
Dorsoduro 3228
30100 Venezia
Tel: +39-041-523-3035
Fax: +39-041-522-4527
lagunabb@tin.it
www.lagunab.com
Visits by appointment only.

AZIENDA AGRICOLA VISTORTA
33077 Vistorta di Sacile (PN)
Tel: +39-043-471-135
Fax: +39-043-473-4878
www.vistorta.it
Visits by appointment only.

I met Brandino and Marie when I was organizing the cooking program for the Hotel Cipriani. There were always winemakers at our dinners, and Primo and Annalisa Franco (page 85) brought their divine Prosecco—and their friends Brandino and Marie, who came with some of his wine and her tumblers. I went to visit her studio the next day, was completely smitten with the glassware, and did some serious shopping. We followed up with a visit to Vistorta, a model farm since the 1800s as well as a vineyard. We had lunch, served by white-gloved waiters in a frescoed dining room, begun with wedges of Marie's Spaghetti Tart, after which we feasted on the estate's produce and drank Vistorta's wonderful merlot.

I use Marie's tumblers for water glasses and as vases for flowers. I drink Brandino's merlot whenever I can. And I'm wild about Marie's recipe for Spaghetti Tart, although, unlike Marie, I make it with extra virgin instead of butter.

SPAGHETTI TART

SERVES 6 TO 8

½ cup plus 1 tablespoon butter or extra virgin

½ cup pine nuts

3 tablespoons coarse sea salt

14–16 ounces spaghetti

Pinch of saffron threads

¼ cup black olives, pitted and roughly chopped

2 tablespoons salt-packed capers, rinsed (optional)

¾ cup diced ham

¼ cup grated Parmigiano-Reggiano cheese

Gently heat 1 tablespoon butter or oil and lightly toast the pine nuts. Set aside.

Bring 5 to 6 quarts of water to a rolling boil, add 3 tablespoons salt, and add the spaghetti. Cook a few minutes less than usual, fairly al dente.

Put the saffron threads into a small cup and cover with 2 tablespoons pasta-cooking water.

Drain the pasta, reserving ¼ cup cooking water. Toss the pasta in a bowl with 7 tablespoons butter, the saffron and its liquid, the olives, capers (if you like), ham, and Parmigiano-Reggiano. If the mixture seems too dry, add some of the reserved pasta-cooking water.

Heat the remaining tablespoon of butter in a large nonstick skillet. Add the pasta, pressing with a spatula to make one even layer. Cook over medium heat until the pasta is crisp, the bottom lightly browned. Slip the pasta onto a plate and invert back into the skillet to cook the second side. Serve hot, cut into wedges.

* * *

Natale and Connie Rusconi

THE EDITOR of an American food magazine who was visiting Italy invited me to meet her in Venice so I could show her the kind of places I wanted to write about. We stayed at the Cipriani since she knew the director, Natale Rusconi, who, I quickly discovered, was charming, amusing, and interested in many of my personal obsessions, including food and wine. He's a member of the Accademia della Cucina Italiana, a most important food association (not just anyone can join; a person must be nominated and approved), and the translator of H. P. Pelleprat's classic *L'art dans la Cuisine*. Natale offered to take us anywhere for lunch. I wanted to visit a place on the island of Cavallino that I'd heard about; he spoke to the concierge, made a reservation, ordered the Cipriani's private launch, and we were off on an adventure in the Venetian lagoon.

HOTEL CIPRIANI AND PALAZZO VENDRAMIN

Giudecca, 10
30133 Venezia
Tel: + 39-041-520-7744
Fax: + 39-041-520-3930
info@hotelcipriani.it
www.hotelcipriani.com
www.trattorialaguna.it
All credit cards accepted.

Our first stop was on the island of Murano, to tour the workshop of a famous sculptor who works with the most Venetian of materials—glass. Next we headed for the island of Cavallino and the restaurant La Laguna, where we had a phenomenal meal. Natale later informed me that the Cipriani's concierge had told him the restaurant was horrible, dirty; but he figured it was my call. I gained his respect, and as a result, Natale asked me to direct the Cipriani's cooking school. Organizing Italians isn't an easy task, but the rewards included staying at the Cipriani for a month in the fall. Linen sheets and superb service made me feel like Eloise at the Plaza.

Natale's a fantastic cook (he'd frequently teach a lesson at the Cipriani Cooking School), and I've tasted some pretty wonderful dishes in his kitchen with his wife Connie including this sauce for spaghetti and spicy onions subjected to lengthy cooking.

SPAGHETTI WITH SPICY ONION-TOMATO SAUCE

SERVES 4

4 garlic cloves, finely chopped

¼ cup extra virgin olive oil

2–4 small dried chili peppers

3 cups coarsely chopped onions

Sea salt

1½ cups fresh tomato pulp, with juice (seeded, coarsely chopped—
   not necessary to peel tomatoes)

12 ounces pasta

Place the chopped garlic in a large heavy-bottomed skillet with the olive oil and chili peppers and cook over low heat until golden.

Add the onions, season with salt, and stir to coat the onions. Cover and cook over lowest heat for about 30 minutes. Add ½ cup hot water, bring to a simmer, lower the heat, and cook for another 10 minutes.

Add the tomatoes to the pan with their juice and cook over lowest heat for another 30 to 40 minutes, adding up to 2 cups of hot water to sauce as it dries out to prevent sticking.

Meanwhile, bring 5 or 6 quarts of water to a rolling boil. Add 3 to 4 tablespoons sea salt and the pasta, and cook until it offers considerable resistance to the tooth, around three-quarters of the package cooking time. Drain the pasta, saving 2 cups of the pasta-cooking water, and add the pasta to the sauce in the skillet. Add some of the reserved pasta water if the sauce seems too dry. Toss well and serve.

* * *

Peter Dipoli

ETER DIPOLI is from Alto Adige. He has a rotund, ruddy-cheeked, Tyrolean look, and he frequently wears a traditional-to-his-area blue apron while working in the vineyards or cellar. When I first met him, he was an apple grower, but he had studied winemaking and was passionate about wine. He opened an enoteca where fine wines—local, regional, Italian, and beyond—and simple food were served, but he has since sold it and now dedicates himself full time to his winery. He makes three wines: Vogler, the local name for a rich, typical sauvignon; Iugum (*yoke* in Latin), a cabernet-merlot blend; and Fihl, the ancient name for the village where it's grown, which is mostly merlot. All are well worth hunting for.

AZIENDA AGRICOLA PETER DIPOLI

Via Villa, 5
39044 Neumarkt Egna (BZ)
Tel: +39-0471-813-400
Fax: +39-0471-813-444
Cell: +39-338-608-1133
info@peterdipoli.com
www.peterdipoli.com

Peter's a great source of information on his area—where to find the best artisanal speck and cheese, which new wineries and restaurants to visit, where to stay—and his website has plenty of tips for food-and-wine-loving travelers to Alto Adige; you can e-mail him for more. Tell him you're a friend and he'll help with accommodations. I love his recipe for leftover meat and boiled potatoes, an Alto Adige version of hash.

LEFTOVER BEEF AND POTATOES

MAIN COURSE

SERVES 4 TO 6

3 medium potatoes

Sea salt

6 tablespoons extra virgin olive oil, or 3 tablespoons extra virgin
    and 3 tablespoons butter

1 onion, chopped

1 pound boiled boneless beef or leftover pot roast,
    cut into bite-size pieces

(recipe continues)

Freshly ground black pepper

¾ cup beef broth (optional)

1 tablespoon minced fresh parsley

1 tablespoon minced fresh chives

Wash the potatoes and boil them in salted water until tender. Drain, cool, peel, and slice ¼ inch thick.

Heat 2 tablespoons of the extra virgin or butter in a nonstick skillet and sauté the potato slices over medium heat until they begin to brown, breaking them up with a wooden spoon but not mashing them.

In another skillet, heat 2 tablespoons extra virgin or butter. Add the chopped onion and cook until it's transparent, around 5 minutes. Add the meat and potatoes, season with pepper, and stir and cook for 6 to 7 minutes. Add the broth, a few tablespoons at a time, if the mixture is too dry. Stir in the parsley and chives, and serve.

Ivan Bertelli and Barbara Aimi

IVAN BERTELLI is the animator of Hostaria da Ivan in *la bassa,* the flatlands of Emilia's Po Valley. His wife, Barbara Aimi, hard at work in the kitchen, is the practical one. At the Salone del Gusto, Slow Food's biennial fair in Torino, Ivan presided over the only restaurant with its own stand, located far from the fair's official osteria. There, Ivan served *salumi* and cheese from his restaurant, wines from friends. I sampled culatello, the most precious cured pork of his region—ground zero for prosciutto production—and humble mortadella, which Ivan calls "bricklayer's culatello," all served with nonstop patter and great enthusiasm. He opened a bottle of Champagne with a knife (instead of a saber, the way they do in France) in one well-practiced stroke, without losing a drop. I was impressed. We met again at VinItaly, the annual Italian wine fair, where Ivan was working at Cavicchioli's (page 65) Lambrusco stand. Why, you might ask, with all the fantastic (and unaffordable) wines of Italy, like Barolo, Barbaresco, and Brunello, there for the sampling, would anyone bother visiting a Lambrusco stand? The attractions are Ivan's ebullient spirit, his quality *salumi,* and "Ivan-ade," a large goblet of Lambrusco, sparkling water, and ice that is the perfect antidote to both physical and palate fatigue after kilometers of winery-packed pavilions. In short, the stand was fun, a rarity at a wine fair. I promised to visit the restaurant.

At Hostaria da Ivan, the entryway bar is stacked with cases of important wine and Champagne, lined with old-fashioned vitrines housing a selection of products like mostarda, sweet and spicy fruit chutney, espresso, and rice, as well as tables with guidebooks and food and wine publications. There's a large dining room on a veranda overlooking the garden, although Ivan sometimes feeds friends in the "cellar" where wine and prosciutto age. The tables are set with the usual stemware, plus a small white porcelain bowl called a *foietta,* the traditional vessel from which to drink Lambrusco. "Hold the *foietta* with index finger in bowl," Ivan explained, "and when your finger is dry, it's time for a refill." Ivan serves a series of traditional dishes like *tosone* (freshly made Parmigiano trim) fried with pancetta, polenta crisps served with herb butter or creamy fatback pesto, braided tortellini, and the osteria's signature dish (recipe from Ivan's mother), Roast Duck with Mostarda. Dinner often concludes in the wine cellar, Ivan knocking off Champagne corks with the handiest utensil—knife, spoon, whatever— and slicing choice salami. Ivan and Barbara have added a few rooms so guests don't have to navigate after an excess of dining and drinking.

HOSTARIA DA IVAN
Via Villa, 73
43010 Fontanelle (PR)
Tel: +39-0521-870-113
Fax: +39-0521-370-191
hostariadaivan@virgilio.it
Closed Mondays and Tuesdays;
closed July 20–August 20.
All credit cards accepted.

Those who can't make the trip to Fontanelle can make the duck and hunt for the mostarda. And maybe even find someone who knows how to saber- or utensil-open sparkling wine to complete the experience.

MAIN COURSE

ROAST DUCK WITH MOSTARDA

SERVES 4 TO 6

1 teaspoon fresh rosemary leaves

1 teaspoon fresh sage leaves

1 tablespoon juniper berries, crushed

3 fresh bay leaves

½ teaspoon grated nutmeg

Sea salt and freshly ground black pepper

1 duck, 5 to 6 pounds

1 cup dry white wine

¾–1 cup mostarda (see Note)

Mince the rosemary, sage, juniper berries, and bay leaves together. Add the nutmeg, salt, and pepper. Rub the duck with this mixture, putting any extra in the duck's cavity. Place in a nonreactive bowl or plastic bag and refrigerate for at least two days.

Remove the duck from the refrigerator and let it come to room temperature. Preheat the oven to 425°F.

Place the duck on a roasting rack in a pan and roast for 45 minutes. Remove the pan from the oven, skim off some but not all the fat, add the wine to the pan, baste the duck, and put it back in the oven for another 45 minutes. (Warning: This may smoke up the kitchen a little.)

Remove the duck from the oven, transfer to a platter, and keep warm. Scrape up the pan juices and pour into a measuring cup. Skim off the fat.

Cut the duck into four pieces and serve with the pan juices and mostarda.

NOTE: Mostarda takes various forms in Italy, whole or puréed fruit or a mix, and spiced with piquant mustard oil. Ivan and Barbara make their own with *anguria bianca,* or white melon, but suggest hunting for the fine mostarda made by Le Tamerici.

Josko and Loredana Sirk

WHEN I WAS EXPLORING the Collio area of Friuli for my book *Eating in Italy,* I was told by my friend Elda Felluga (page 38) about an *agriturismo* (working farm that takes paying guests) north of Gorizia, owned by Josko and Loredana Sirk. Josko and Loredana grow grapes for wine, though less than they used to and probably not enough to comply to the letter of the *agriturismo* law, but I don't think anyone's going to turn them in. They sell a wonderful selection of products from neighboring farms and utilize local produce at Al Cacciatore, their highly regarded trattoria. There, the meals are rustic and the cucina highly traditional, bound to season and territory.

Look for superlative lightly smoked prosciutto, potato or winter squash gnocchi, homemade pasta, hearty soups in the winter, and the house specialty, Roast Veal Shank. The wine list is superb, easy to drink from, and will make guests glad they're staying in one of the fourteen apartments across from the trattoria, each with its own living room, bedroom, kitchen, and bathroom. Furnishings are a mixture of antiques and reproductions, walls are brightly colored and stenciled, mattresses are firm, and most apartments have a *fogolar,* the traditional onion-domed hearth fireplace native to the region. Tennis, swimming, horseback riding, hiking in the woods, and a playground for kids are among the in-between meals activities.

TRATTORIA AL CACCIATORE
Località Subida, 22
34071 Cormons (GO)
Tel: +39-0481-605-31
Fax: +39-0481-616-16
info@lasubida.it
www.lasubida.it
Closed Tuesdays and Wednesdays;
dinner only Mondays, Thursdays,
and Fridays.

LA SUBIDA
Localita' Monte, 22
34071 Cormons (GO)
Tel: +39-0481-605-31
Fax: +39-0481-616-16
info@lasubida.it
www.lasubida.it

ROAST VEAL SHANK

SERVES 6

1 veal shank, hind leg, 4½–5 pounds
2 garlic cloves, split
Sea salt and freshly ground black pepper
1 carrot, roughly chopped
1 large white onion, roughly chopped
3–4 tablespoons extra virgin olive oil
2 ounces salt pork, diced
3–4 tablespoons butter, cut up
2 tablespoons fresh sage leaves
2 pinches dried marjoram
1½–2 cups broth, beef, chicken, or vegetable, kept at a simmer

Preheat the oven to 370°F.

Rub the veal shank with garlic, season it with salt and pepper, and place in a heavy-bottomed roasting pan. Sprinkle the carrot and onion around the meat, pour the extra virgin over the meat, then scatter the salt pork, bits of butter, and herbs over the meat. Roast for 20 to 25 minutes, or until lightly colored.

Turn the meat over and roast for another 20 to 25 minutes. Then turn the heat down to 300°F and roast for another 30 minutes.

Turn meat again, and, if the vegetables are getting very colored, add ½ cup broth. Turn the meat every 30 minutes, adding ½ cup simmering broth, if necessary, each time. Cook for a total of 3 to 3½ hours or until meat is fork-tender.

Serve the veal shank standing up (big part down) and spoon the pan juices around it. Carve slices parallel to the bone.

* * *

Mauro Lorenzon

M AURO LORENZON is a madman-sommelier—a partner at a wine bar in Venice called Mascareta, the down-the-lane annex of Osteria al Mascaron (page 45). He is renowned for his skill with a saber— he lops off the tops of sparkling wine bottles with a flourish that never fails to enchant. He founded the enoiteca association of wine bars, adding an *i* to the word *enoteca* to denote wine bars that offer an ultra-hospitable attitude in addition to super extra virgin and wine selections. Clad in a leather apron, Mauro himself is a perfect enoiteca host, dispensing wine with a manic spirit that is simply impossible to resist, and he knows more about wine than almost anyone else I know. Mauro uses a large wineglass as a megaphone, a creative inspiration born of necessity when he was once asked to speak about wine in front of a restless group of drinkers. "*Attenzione!!*" Mauro thunders into his crystal goblet, and he gets attention because he's spent lots of time visiting wineries and drinking, not just tasting and spitting. Mauro's also a master oyster shucker—it must have something to do with all that sparkling wine he sabers open.

MASCARETA
Castello, 5183
Calle Lunga Santa Maria Formosa
30100 Venezia
Tel/Fax: +39-041-523-0744
lorenzon.mauro@virgilio.it
Open 7 P.M.–2 A.M.; closed
Wednesdays and Thursdays.
All credit cards accepted.

Mauro explains his philosophy as "the certainty of doubt," which is how I approached his recipe, given the enchanting enough name of *Scquacquaciò di Mare,* or "watery mess" of seafood. It's the kind of dish you can make after excessive wine consumption, as it doesn't require a lot of skill or effort. Mauro serves it with soft polenta, but it's so quick and easy (unlike polenta) that I often make it as a main course without the polenta. Be sure to sop up the sauce with bread—appropriate behavior that's known in Italy as *la scarpetta.*

WATERY MESS SEAFOOD

SERVES 4

2 teaspoons fine sea salt

3 cups filtered water

1–1½ pounds Manila clams, cockles, and/or mussels

½ pound shrimp, squid, cuttlefish, scallops, or fish fillets in chunks

2 tablespoons extra virgin olive oil

2 garlic cloves, peeled

1 chili pepper or a pinch of red pepper flakes

2 tablespoons white wine

2 tablespoons white wine vinegar

¼ cup tomato sauce

1 tablespoon chopped fresh parsley

Rustic county-style bread or polenta

Dissolve the sea salt in the water and soak the Manila clams in the reconstituted sea water for at least 15 minutes. Scrub the mussels and remove the beards; slice the squid or cuttlefish into strips.

Heat the extra virgin in a large skillet over high heat. Add the garlic and chili pepper, and when the garlic begins to color, add the clams and/or mussels. Pile the rest of the fish on top of the shells. Add the wine, vinegar, and tomato sauce, then cover and cook for 5 to 10 minutes or until the mussels are open.

Remove all the fish and seafood to a serving platter, reduce the sauce for a few minutes, and pour over the seafood. Sprinkle with the parsley and serve with bread or polenta.

Carla and Giovanni Galli

ONCE I HAD TASTED Carla and Giovanni's fantastic *balsamico*, I had to visit their *acetaia* outside of Modena, where the vinegar was made and aged. In their attic we tasted the balsamic in the official balsamic style, licking precious drops of the ancient vinegar that were dribbled from a glass wand onto the back of the hand. It's a far cry from the "instant" balsamic vinegar that's found in supermarkets and restaurants all over the world.

ACETAIA GALLI
Via Albareto, 452
41100 Modena (RE)
Tel: +39-059-251-094
Visits by appointment only.

When I order their traditional *balsamico,* Carla and Giovanni bring it to me personally, planning the delivery to coincide with interesting art exhibitions in Florence. Carla and I speak frequently discussing everything from the bureaucratic problems traditional producers face in fighting the giant industrial interests, to mutual friends and restaurants in the Modena area, to new ways to use her excellent product. Traditional balsamic vinegar should always be used as a condiment. Never cook with it; rather, drizzle it on dishes after they've been cooked. Try a bit on a baked

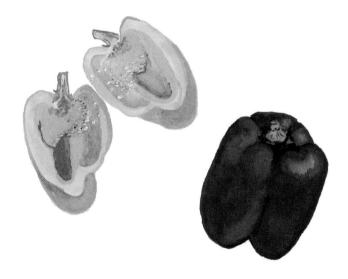

or boiled potato, a frittata, with chunks of Parmigiano-Reggiano or peperonata—the latter an unusual suggestion that's become a classic in my kitchen. Don't even think about trying this with the industrial stuff.

SIDE DISH

STEWED PEPPERS WITH BALSAMIC VINEGAR

SERVES 4 TO 8

1 large red onion, chopped
1–2 garlic cloves, chopped
1 small carrot, chopped
3 tablespoons extra virgin olive oil
4–5 yellow and/or red bell peppers, seeded and cut into strips
½ cup fresh tomato pulp (chopped peeled and seeded tomato)
1 teaspoon chopped flat-leaf parsley
1½–2 cups boiling water
Sea salt and freshly ground black pepper
1 teaspoon traditional balsamic vinegar from Modena

Put the onion, garlic, and carrot in a 4-quart heavy-bottomed pot and drizzle with extra virgin. Stir to coat the vegetables with oil and place the pot over medium heat. Cook until the onions are soft but not brown.

Add the peppers, tomato pulp, parsley, and 1 cup boiling water. Season lightly with salt and pepper, lower the heat, and simmer for 20 to 25 minutes or until the peppers are soft. Add up to 1 cup boiling water if peppers become too dry.

Transfer the peppers to a serving dish and cool. Serve at room temperature, drizzled with traditional balsamic vinegar. (Of course Carla uses her own production.)

* * *

Giovanni and Carlo Fiori

M Y FIRST ENCOUNTER with Giovanni Fiori and his father, Carlo, was at a trade fair with a group of Piemontese food artisans brought together by Giacomo Bologna, a strong believer in the synergy of regional producers. Giovanni and his father select artisanal cheese from all over Italy for their ripening cellars, and they supply a vast array of first-rate, hard-to-find cheeses to restaurants and shops throughout the country and internationally. Their cheese was paired with Roberto Santopietro's (page 80) *cognà* fall fruit chutney, a perfect match and a convincing argument for a visit to the Guffanti establishment in Arona, on the Piemonte side of Lago Maggiore.

LUIGI GUFFANTI DI FIORI GIOVANNI & C. S.A.S.
Via Milano, 140
28041 Arona (NO)
Tel: +39-0322-242-038
Fax: +39-0322-241-356
info@guffantiformaggi.com
www.guffantiformaggi.com
Visits by appointment only.

Giovanni showed me the maze of rooms in their aging cellars, where shelves of cheese, cheese, and more cheese stretch from floor to ceiling. He introduced me to each one like an old friend, reciting provenance, artisan, kind of milk, age, optimal ripeness. One entire room was filled with wheels of Parmigiano aged for 24, 36, even 48 months, some labeled with the names of the restaurants that had purchased them and left them to be aged by Guffanti. Huge walk-in refrigerators, each with a different temperature and humidity level, were filled with fresh cheese. Giovanni explained that the company was founded in 1976 by his great-grandfather Luigi Guffanti, who aged his Gorgonzola in an abandoned silver mine, achieving perfection and success. The passion for cheese grew with each generation of Guffantis, as did the selection of cheeses they sell.

After my tour, Giovanni took me home for a cheese-tasting lunch. We tasted in flights, starting with mild cheese eaten plain and then with condiments like *cognà* and chestnut honey before moving on to aged cheese and finally the blues. I was truly impressed by three versions of Gorgonzola—creamy, tangy, and aged 200 days. After tasting twenty different cheeses I was happy to see some greens on the table, topped with melty fatback and smoky ricotta. I asked for the recipe, hoping I'd be able to reproduce it at home, even if Giovanni's smoked ricotta wasn't available. I've re-created the flavor with a blend of fresh smoky cheese and ricotta. Giovanni says that this mixture is great spread on toast or paired with boiled or baked potatoes.

SIDE DISH

"FORTIFIED" RICOTTA SALAD

SERVES 4 TO 6

1 cup Ossolana ricotta (or, since you'll probably never find this
    cheese, ½ cup grated fresh smoked mozzarella combined with
    ½ cup ricotta)
2 tablespoons heavy cream
Chili pepper to taste
Abundant freshly ground black pepper
Sea salt
8–12 thin slices lardo, or slices bacon, or other cured pork product
1–1½ cups cleaned salad greens
2–3 tablespoons extra virgin olive oil
½ teaspoon red wine vinegar

Combine the ricotta, cream, chili pepper, and black pepper and mash with a fork to form a smooth paste. Season with salt and refrigerate for at least 3 hours.

Sauté the lardo or cured pork product and drain on paper towels.

Dress the salad with extra virgin, vinegar, salt and pepper. Divide among four to six plates. Top each salad with two slices of crisp pork, then the ricotta. Serve immediately.

*   *   *

Angela Lorenz; Gianni and Cosimo Figliomeni

ANGELA LORENZ studied art in Bologna, where she met and married Calabrian architecture student Gianni Figliomeni. Together they convinced Gianni's brother Cosimo to open a gelateria there. They called it Gelatauro, a nod to the Byzantine mosaic of a bull in nearby Ravenna's Basilica of San Vitale, as well as the street, Via San Vitale. Angela has reinterpreted this mosaic with the bull's horns as ice cream cones, and painted watercolors of fruit mosaics that are as impressive as Cosimo's gelato: both are well worth the trip to Bologna. Original flavor combinations (and names) like Principe di Calabria (jasmine and bergamot), Crema del Pastore (custard with honey, ricotta, and coffee), and Re delle due Sicilie (pistachio, almond, and sponge cake) are made with all-natural seasonal flavors and colors—no phosphorescent green pistachio! Cosimo also makes more than a dozen kinds of chocolate gelato, rotating different chocolates and different bean percentages. In the winter months, citrus fruit is shipped from the family's grove in Calabria.

IL GELATAURO
Via San Vitale, 82/b
40100 Bologna
Tel: +39-051-230-049
aslorenz@crocker.com
www.gelatauro.com
www.angelalorenzartistsbooks.com
Closed Mondays.

With success has come a larger location down the street, a former bakery. Gianni has joined his brother at Gelatauro, and introduced new products, like chocolate and pastry. Gelatauro's cookies and cakes are flavored with southern Italian ingredients, like concentrated fig *mosto* (must), candied fruit, rose water, and nuts, but Angela's influence is strong, reflected in international ingredients like candied Australian ginger, the emphasis on organic, and her conceptual art installations that relate the history of gelato, coffee, and chocolate.

I'm wild about their orange gelato, but it's made with carob flour, not an easy ingredient to find, so I offer here their recipe for candied ginger biscotti. Like mini-scones, these are greatly appreciated in my kitchen, with a glass of Vin Santo for dessert. Or even Sunday brunch.

DESSERT

GINGER APRICOT BISCOTTI

MAKES APPROXIMATELY 20 COOKIES

3½ cups soft wheat flour (Italian "00" or White Lily flour)

2 teaspoons baking powder

¼ cup plus 1 tablespoon raw (Demerara) sugar

¼ teaspoon fine sea salt

3 tablespoons unsalted butter, chilled

⅔ cup chopped candied ginger

½ cup chopped dried apricots

½ medium apple, peeled, cored, and chopped

3 eggs

⅔ cup heavy cream

Preheat the oven to 425°F.

Combine the flour, baking powder, sugar, and salt in a bowl. Cut the chilled butter into the flour and sugar mixture (or pulse in food processor). Add the chopped ginger, apricots, and apple to the flour and sugar mixture.

Beat the eggs and cream together in another bowl. Add the egg-cream mixture to the batter and mix quickly, until the dough comes together.

Transfer the dough to a piece of parchment paper, pat out to an 8 by 10-inch rectangle around ¾ inch thick. Cut into 2½-inch squares.

Bake the biscotti on a parchment-lined baking sheet for 12 to 15 minutes or until lightly browned.

Claudio, Sandro, Federica, Liliana, and Piergiorgio Cavicchioli

I MET CLAUDIO, Sandro, and Federica Cavicchioli at VinItaly, the annual wine fair in Verona. The Cavicchiolis are fun, just like their wine, a deliciously grapey Lambrusco which, mixed with sparkling water and ice and served in large goblets, makes a refreshing thirst-quencher for palates fatigued by serious wine tasting.

The invitation to the Cavicchiolis' traditional Emilian party (kill a pig, have a butcher turn it into all its respective *salumi* and fresh pork cuts, and then cook and serve everything to all your friends) read *"Maiale si nasce, salame si diventa"* (Pigs are born, salami is created), an amusing double meaning since *salami* also means "idiots" in Italian. My assistant Jenn and I spent the evening in the area so we could watch the action that began at 7 A.M. We arrived early, and three butchers and their helpers had already set up workstations with huge pots of water on burners and knives arranged just so. But the pigs were late, so Federica drove us to her par-

CANTINE CAVICCHIOLI U. E FIGLI S.R.L.

Offices:

Piazza Gramsci, 9

41030 San Prospero (MO)

Tel: + 39-059-812411

Fax: + 39-059-812424

Wine Cellar:

Via Nazionale, 118

41030 Sorbara (MO)

cantine@cavicchioli.it

www.cavicchioli.it

Visits by appointment only.

ents' house to pick up some platters and cookies that her mother had made for the party. We made it back to the kitchen, schlepping platters and cookies, in time to watch the butchers dismantle the pigs, cutting slabs of meat and chops, and boiling the cotechino sausage they'd made the day before. Outside a cauldron bubbled with pork skin and attached fat; the end of the skin was pressed in a special vise to produce the freshest and best *ciccioli* cracklings I've ever tasted.

The party began around lunchtime and concluded with breakfast the next morning. Cavicchioli Lambrusco flowed and friends and clients feasted on *salumi,* pasta, grilled cuts of pork, and desserts including Mom's cookies, which disappeared quickly. Jenn snagged the recipe, which includes a direct translation of her egg-beating instructions.

DESSERT

AMARETTI COOKIES

MAKES APPROXIMATELY 30 COOKIES

10 ounces almonds, peeled and finely chopped

1½ cups sugar less 1 tablespoon

3 egg whites

Pinch of sea salt

Preheat the oven to 300°F. Cover a baking sheet with a piece of parchment paper.

Mix the almonds and sugar well. Beat the egg whites to clouds of snow (or soft peaks) with the salt, then slowly fold them into the sugar mixture. Drop tablespoonfuls of the batter onto the prepared baking sheet, with ample space between.

Bake for 22 to 28 minutes or until golden brown. (If you are baking more than one cookie sheet at a time, you may need to rotate the pans halfway through cooking.) Transfer the cookies to a wire rack to cool.

Silvano, Cristina, Gianni, Pietro, and Emilio Domenis

I HAD NEVER BEEN a big fan of grappa. The local tradition of using the leftovers of winemaking to produce a product something like moonshine has become a big business that's mostly about important winery labels and fancy bottles. An exception to the rule, however, is the grappa made by Domenis—a family business with two brothers and their children involved in distilling and marketing their fine products. I had already fallen in love with their Storica line of grappa when I met Cristina Domenis at the VinItaly wine fair. Distilled in a discontinuous copper still, the grappa is made from the very best pomace and is distilled at a lower temperature to preserve flavors.

DISTILLERIA DOMENIS S.R.L.
Via Darnazzacco, 30
33043 Cividale del Friuli (UD)
Tel: +39-0432-73-1023
Fax: + 39-0432-701-153
domenis@domenis.it
www.domenis.com
Visits by appointment only.

The Domenis family distilled grappa even before their arrival in Friuli in 1898, prior to the enactment of the law governing the production of grappa. They distill and age many kinds of grappa and grape brandy, including kosher and organic. I bonded with Storica Nera (made with red grape pomace), which in addition to the traditional bottle can be purchased in adorable black cigarette-pack-like flip-top boxes, each containing eight red-plastic-topped 5 ml vials—perfect for emergencies and gifts. I ordered cartons.

I'm totally in love with Cristina's recipe for pan-roasted gubana, which I make at home substituting panettone or pandoro for the delicious but hard-to-find Friulian sweetbread. Any sweet eggy yeast bread (or even challah) will do nicely, too. The grappa wets the bread and makes it custardy, the heat evaporates some of the grappa's alcohol, and the sugar caramelizes to form an irregular sweet, crisp coating. With only three ingredients, all easy enough to have on hand, it's a perfect, almost effortless dessert to whip up at the last minute. If you're using pandoro or panettone, slice the loaf horizontally, producing a "star" or round.

GRILLED, GRAPPA-ED SWEETBREAD

SERVES 6

3 slices gubana, 1 slice panettone or pandoro, or 6 slices sweet yeast
    bread, all 1½ inches thick
¼–¾ cup grappa, preferably Domenis Storica Nera
½–¾ cup sugar
1 tablespoon butter

Drizzle the bread slices with half the grappa, then sprinkle with half the sugar. Generously butter a large nonstick or cast-iron skillet.

Heat the skillet over high heat, and when it's hot, put the slices, sugar side down, into the skillet. Cook for a few minutes to caramelize the sugar and heat the bread.

While the slices are cooking, drizzle the remaining grappa on the upper side of the slices, then sprinkle them with the remaining sugar. Carefully turn the slices over in the skillet with a plastic spatula and cook on the second side for a minute, to caramelize the sugar. Remove from the heat. Repeat with remaining slices. Using a large, sharp knife, cut gubana slices in half, the pandoro or panettone into wedges, and serve immediately.

*   *   *

Cesare and Enrico Bardini

WHEN I TASTED Cesare Bardini's *marrons glacés* at a trade fair I was impressed with their quality—and the cool drawings on the packaging. He came to visit me in Florence to tell me why Agrimontana's *marrons glacés* and preserves were the best in the world. After a lengthy discussion about chestnuts—the difference between *marroni* and *castagne,* as well as the use of fermentation to develop flavor and the candying process—we had a tasting, The *marrons glacés* tasted like chestnuts, not cloying like most, while the preserves tasted true to their ingredients and not overcooked, the best I'd ever tried. When I tried the candied sour cherries, I became a true believer; they were amazing and ultra-cherry-ish.

I later visited the factory to attend a seminar on gelato making, since Agrimontana makes a line of products—chestnut, hazelnut, pistachio, and fruit purées—for gelaterie. Cesare's brother Enrico showed me the copper cauldrons (copper is a better conductor of heat—ingredients cook at a lower temperature, preserving the flavors) and the high-tech, hygienic environment in which Agrimontana's products are made. The tasting room was lined with beautiful fruit etchings by Gianni Gallo, which are reproduced on their labels.

Though the gelato seminar turned out to be a bust, I did go home with more of Agrimontana's fabulous sour cherries. I love the Tuscan combination of chocolate gelato, candied sour cherries, and whipped cream, but I'm also partial to this palate-cleansing pre-dessert inspired by my friends at Oasis (page 228), so I included both. Do search out a source for really good candied cherries (don't even think maraschino). To learn about Agrimontana's fine products, log on to www.agrimontana.it.

AZIENDA AGRIMONTANA

Località Ponte della Sale

12011 Borgo S. Dalmazzo (CN)

Tel: +39-0171-261-157

Fax: +39-0171-261-670

agrimontana@agrimontana.it

www.agrimontana.it/en/welcome.html

Visits by appointment only.

CANDIED SOUR CHERRIES WITH YOGURT

SERVES 4 TO 6

4–6 tablespoons whole-milk, finest-quality plain yogurt
4–6 Agrimontana candied sour cherries and their syrup

Put a tablespoonful of yogurt on attractive large dessert spoons, top each with a sour cherry, and add a drizzle of its syrup.

HARLEQUIN SUNDAE

SERVES 4 TO 6

½ cup heavy cream, chilled
1 teaspoon superfine sugar
4–6 large scoops quality chocolate ice cream (passionate or
    obsessive cooks should make their own chocolate gelato)
4–6 spoonfuls Agrimontana candied sour cherries in syrup

Whip the cream until it forms soft peaks, then gently stir in the sugar.

Scoop the ice cream into individual serving dishes. Drizzle a spoonful of the sour cherries and their syrup over the ice cream, and top each serving with a blob of whipped cream. Drizzle the cream with a little cherry syrup and serve.

* * *

Giannola, Benito, Cristina, Antonella, and Elisabetta Nonino

NONINO DISTILLATORI

33050 Percoto (UD)

Tel: +39-0432-676-331

Fax: +39-0432-676-038

info@nonino.it

www.nonino.it

Visits by appointment only.

W E MET because I was on a mission to purchase one of Nonino's beautiful mouth-blown decanters, with the design of a cluster of grapes melded into the glass. Friends, the Wags, had fallen in love with the bottle and its product, grappa made from Picolit, a rare grape from Friuli. The Wags joined me for the quest, and we traveled to the village of Percoto, to the Nonino distillery. I met Giannola, her husband, Benito, and their daughters, Cristina, Elisabetta, and Antonella. We toured the distillery, with its huge copper stills steaming away and big piles of grape pomace (leftover skins and seeds from the winemaking process); the air was perfumed with the intoxicating scent of just-born grappa.

Giannola told me her story. Whenever she'd go out for dinner with friends, no one ever wanted to finish the meal with her grappa, considered at that time to be a low-life liquor with a moonshine-type reputation. She and Benito decided to distill pomace from the finest, rarest regional grape, Picolit, then package it in attractive glass beakers with silver-topped stoppers, with tags on them written by hand and tied with red yarn—a far cry from the contents and packaging of the rustic grappa most consumers were used to. She started the grappa revolution, and now fancy bottles and single-grape grappa are the norm. Giannola and Benito then decided to distill grapes (not pomace), a novel idea in Friuli, and call it UE, regional dialect for grape. Cristina, Antonella, and Elisabetta, now grown up, had ideas of their own. They decided to age UE in barriques, producing the cognac-like product, and to also distill honey and call it Gioiello (Jewel). It's now impossible to find a fine restaurant or bar anywhere in Italy (and most of the rest of the world, too) that doesn't have a bottle of one of the Nonino distillates. Whenever I'm in Friuli I have to visit the Nonino family—Giannola has taken me shopping, sung me regional folksongs, told me stories, invited me to lunch with her family. And she has served this delicious dessert, made with Gioiello, her daughters' honey distillate. If you can't find it, use any of the Nonino grappa products.

DESSERT

HONEY DISTILLATE SEMIFREDDO

SERVES 6 TO 8

3 eggs, at room temperature (see Note)
Pinch of fine sea salt
½ cup plus 1 tablespoon superfine sugar
1½ cups heavy cream, chilled
¼ cup Gioiello honey distillate or grappa
2–3 tablespoons honey, for garnish

Separate the egg yolks from the whites. Beat the whites with a pinch of salt and 5 tablespoons sugar until very stiff.

Beat the egg yolks with the remaining ¼ cup sugar until thick and pale yellow.

Whip the cream until stiff.

Fold the beaten whites into the egg yolk mixture. Stir the honey distillate into the whipped cream. Fold the whipped cream into the egg mixture and transfer to a 2-quart loaf pan. Freeze overnight, or at least 12 hours.

To serve, warm the sides and bottom of the loaf pan with a hot sponge, then run a knife around the edges and unmold the loaf onto a clean cutting board. Slice the loaf into individual servings and drizzle the slices with honey.

NOTE: This dessert contains raw eggs, and is not appropriate for pregnant women, immuno-compromised individuals, the very young, or the elderly.

Fausto, Franca, and Giuseppina Maculan

WHILE RESEARCHING the first edition of my guidebook *Eating in Italy*, I interviewed Fausto Maculan and his sister Franca at the VinItaly wine fair, asking for regional intelligence, gastronomic and otherwise. Like me, Franca was active in the Donne del Vino, a networking association of women in the Italian wine world, and Fausto was a wealth of information; his wines were also among the best in the region and he was fun. So when they invited me to visit the Maculan winery, located in the center of the town of Breganze, not far from Venice, I was delighted.

AZIENDA AGRICOLA MACULAN
Via Castelletto, 3
36042 Breganze (VI)
Tel: +39-0445-873-733
Fax: +39-0445-300-149
fausto@maculan.net
www.maculan.net
Visits by appointment only.

The winery has high-tech computer systems that control the stainless-steel tanks, a dramatically lit brick cellar of barriques, and an attic hung with ropes of drying grapes that are used to make Torcolato, Maculan's lush dessert wine. During our lunch, prepared by Fausto and Franca's mother, Giuseppina, I had a chance to taste Maculan's impressive wines at the table. For dessert, Fausto poured glasses of Torcolato—amber-colored, full-bodied, elegant, and floral with the aroma of honey. Giuseppina paired it with a rustic bread pudding made from leftover bread turned into crumbs, studded with cooked apples, pears, and raisins soaked in Torcolato. Fausto says it's at its best prepared a day in advance. Visit the Maculan website to take a virtual tour of the vineyard or visit the winery the next time you're in Venice. Either way, seek out Maculan's fine wines.

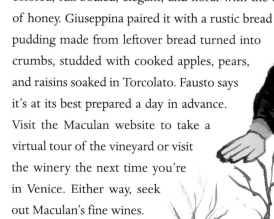

MOM'S FRUIT AND RAISIN BREAD PUDDING

SERVES 6 TO 8

1⅓ cups raisins

1⅓ cups Torcolato, Dindarello, or other fine dessert wine

4 cups milk

1 teaspoon vanilla extract

¼ teaspoon ground cinnamon

2 cups plus 2 tablespoons fresh bread crumbs

Around 12 ounces pears, peeled and sliced

Around 12 ounces apples, peeled and sliced

½ cup unsalted butter, plus more for greasing the pan

1½ cups superfine sugar

3 eggs

Grated zest of 1 lemon

¼ teaspoon sea salt

Confectioners' sugar, for dusting

Soak the raisins in the wine overnight or up to 12 hours, until they absorb almost all the wine.

Heat the milk, then add the vanilla and cinnamon. Put 2 cups of the bread crumbs in a bowl and add the hot milk.

Cook the pears and apples in a saucepan with the butter and superfine sugar over medium-low heat until completely soft, 30 to 45 minutes; they will form a chunky purée.

Preheat the oven to 400°F. Line the bottom of a 10-inch springform pan with parchment paper. Lightly butter the paper and the sides of the pan. Dust the bottom and sides of the pan with the remaining 2 tablespoons bread crumbs.

Beat the eggs in a large bowl. Add the soaked bread and milk mixture and stir to combine. Then add the fruit purée, soaked raisins, lemon zest, and salt. Mix well. Pour into the prepared pan and bake for 35 to 40 minutes, until golden brown. Cool, remove from springform pan, and dust with confectioners' sugar.

Cesare Giaccone and Don Camera

I MET CESARE GIACCONE, one of Piemonte's great chefs, at his restaurant, Il Cacciatore, in Albaretto Torre. I had a choice seat in the dining room, where I could watch Cesare cooking, keep an eye on the spit-roasting kid, and observe truffles being shaved with abandon over many diners' dishes. Cesare was making Zabaione, whisking eggs in a copper pot with a rounded bottom and moving it on and off the heat in a graceful ballet of a preparation. The Zabaione was the lightest, fluffiest I'd ever tasted, served warm with a plate-size cookie that was broken at the table with a hammer.

DA CESARE—
L'ANGOLO
DI PARADISO
Via Umberto, 12
12050 Albaretto Torre (CN)
Tel: +39-0173-520-141
Fax: +39-0173-520-147
Closed all day Tuesday and
Wednesday, all January and
February, and one week in July.
Call ahead for reservations.
No credit cards.

After dinner, Cesare took me to visit his vinegar works and meet his horse. He illuminated the way with a lighter. I expressed admiration for his superb Zabaione, and he told me he learned it from the village priest, Don Camera. He promised to arrange an introduction, which is how I learned the secrets of Cesare's Zabaione. They are as follows: Always use an odd number of egg yolks ("That's the way it's done," Don Camera told me when I asked why) and flavor it with Moscato d'Asti instead of the typical Marsala. Cesare beats his Zabaione in a special tin-lined copper pot with a balloon whisk, but I've found that any rounded bowl works well (use a potholder because it will get hot). I use the whisk attachment for my immersion mixer, which seems to work faster than a hand mixer. Cesare works over high heat, never stops whisking, and moves the pot off and back on the heat, but more than thirty years of experience have made him a master; home cooks may prefer the slower-but-surer method of using medium heat the whole time, moving the pot or bowl off the heat only if necessary.

DESSERT

ZABAIONE

SERVES 4

3 egg yolks, at room temperature
3 tablespoons sugar
3 tablespoons Moscato d'Asti wine
Butter or hazelnut cookies or fresh fruit or berries

Place the egg yolks, sugar, and Moscato d'Asti in a 1½- or 2-quart pot (copper is nice but not essential). Begin beating at high speed with a mixer until foamy. Place over medium heat and continue beating (those who would like to follow Cesare's example and use high heat should be cautious, ready to shift the pot or bowl frequently). The mixture will grow greatly in volume and thicken. When the mixture feels warm, remove the pot from the heat and continue beating, then place back over the heat, beating the whole time. Continue removing the pot from the heat when it seems to be heating up too much. Practice makes perfect. The Zabaione will be thick and foamy, warm but not hot to the touch.

Serve in individual glass serving bowls with the cookies on the side, or over berries or sliced fresh soft ripe fruit such as peaches or mango.

* * *

Diane Rankin and Cesare Benelli

ɪN 1986, a wine rep told me about a new restaurant in Venice owned and run by a Venetian chef and his American wife. I took a train to Venice as soon as I could, and I have been going back to Al Covo ever since. Chef Cesare Benelli is handsome, is obsessed with the fish and seafood of the Venetian lagoon, and has been into wine since before the restaurants of Venice (a city without cellars) developed better selections. His Texan wife, Diane Rankin, speaks Italian with a Venetian accent, works the dining rooms, and prepares desserts.

Al Covo has two small dining rooms (the nonsmoking one was the American room until all restaurants in Italy banned smoking) whose bare-brick walls are decorated with vintage Venetian glass and contemporary art. The wine list is a joy, well priced, and loaded with unknown gems, especially from Veneto and Friuli. I've visited the restaurant in all seasons, feasting on soft-shell crabs and the season's first *castraure* (wild

RISTORANTE AL COVO

Campiello della Pescaria
Castello, 3968
30122 Venezia
Vaporetto stop: San Zaccaria
Tel/Fax: +39-041-522-3812
www.ristorantealcovo.com
Closed Wednesday and Thursday,
January 7–February 10, and one
week in August. All credit cards
accepted.

artichokes), or helping Diane and Cesare clean piles of gray shrimp. I've tasted wines with Cesare and his friends Gigi (page 45) and Mauro (page 57) and closed the restaurant many evenings. After lunch at Al Covo, I've come close to missing the train back to Florence more than once, and raced to the station by water taxi. It was Cesare who turned me on to Latini pasta, and I'll be grateful forever. He taught me one of the secrets for making great risotto: the rice, when cooked with extra virgin over high heat, has to make whistling sounds; after that, wine is added to "shock" the mixture, then broth is added as usual.

Cesare and Diane have a *foresteria* guest apartment close to the restaurant with two bedrooms, bath, kitchen, satellite TV, Internet connection, air-conditioning, and a wine refrigerator. It's rented by the day at prices that run far less than a hotel room. Cesare's fish preparations are simple and ingredient driven, but although I've tried to reproduce his dishes, they are not the same without the sweet-tasting seafood from the Venetian lagoon. Instead, I asked Diane for her recipe for Pear Cake with Grappa Sauce, which is always on the menu at Al Covo.

PEAR CAKE WITH GRAPPA SAUCE

DESSERT

SERVES 6 TO 8

PEAR CAKE

Oil for greasing the baking pan

1¼ cups soft wheat flour (Italian "00" or White Lily flour),
   plus more for dusting the pan

1½ teaspoons baking powder

½ cup unsalted butter, at room temperature

1¼ cups sugar

1 teaspoon ground cinnamon

3 large eggs, at room temperature

2 tablespoons milk

1 tablespoon grappa

3 large pears, peeled, cored, and cut into 1-inch chunks

10–12 prunes, pitted and chopped into 1-inch pieces

½ cup pine nuts, toasted lightly and cooled

GRAPPA SAUCE

1 large egg

¼ cup plus 2 tablespoons sugar

2 tablespoons unsalted butter

1 teaspoon ground cinnamon

½ cup plus 2 tablespoons heavy cream, chilled

1 tablespoon grappa

Preheat the oven to 375°F. Lightly oil and flour a 10-inch springform pan, knocking out excess flour.

Make the cake. Combine the flour and baking powder in a bowl. In another bowl, beat the butter with 1 cup and 2 tablespoons sugar and the cinnamon until light and fluffy. Add the eggs, one at a time, beating well after each addition, then beat in the milk and grappa.

Fold the flour into the egg mixture. Fold the pears, prunes, and pine nuts into the batter and scrape into the prepared pan. Sprinkle the top with the remaining 2 tablespoons sugar. Bake for 45 to 50 minutes. A tester should show moist crumbs. Cool on a rack, then remove sides of the pan.

While the cake cools, make the grappa sauce. In a mixing bowl, beat the egg and sugar until thick and pale. Melt the butter in a double boiler or metal bowl set over a pan of simmering water and stir in the egg mixture and cinnamon. Cook the sauce, stirring constantly, until thickened and hot, 10 to 15 minutes, or to 165°F. Remove the bowl from the pan, stir in the cream, and chill.

Strain the sauce through a sieve to remove any lumps and add the grappa. Warm the sauce to serve over the cake.

Roberto, Margherita, Carlo, Giacomo, and Ginevra Santopietro

AZIENDA AGRICOLA IL MONGETTO

Cascina Mongetto, 10
15049 Vignale Monferrato (AL)
Tel: +39-0142-933-442
Fax: +39-0142-933-469
info@mongetto.it
www.mongetto.it
Visits by appointment only.

DRÉ CASTÈ IL MONGETTO

Via Piave, 2
15049 Vignale Monferrato (AL)
Tel/Fax: +39-0142-933-442
info@mongetto.it
www.mongetto.it

THE SANTOPIETRO FAMILY—Carlo and his brother Roberto, moved to Piemonte from Milan and revitalized their farm in the province of Alessandria. Called Il Mongetto, it has new vineyards, heirloom fruit trees, hazelnuts, corn for polenta, and spicy cherry peppers. They also created a line of jarred products that includes anchovy- and caper-stuffed peppers, bagna cauda garlic and anchovy dip, and *Mostarda d'Uva*, a traditional Piemontese fall fruit chutney. I visited the factory and was impressed by all the work done by hand, the quality ingredients—Spanish anchovies, great extra virgin, capers from Pantelleria—and the superior flavors of the products. I retired to their shabby-chic *agriturismo* farm, Dré Castè, which means "behind the castle" in dialect, despite the fact that there's no castle nearby. An eighteenth-century building, with frescoes decorating many of the ceilings, houses the guests. Five-course meals, accompanied by Il Mongetto's outstanding red wines, are available for guests with advance notice; those not staying at the farm can reserve to dine on weekends. Breakfast doesn't get much better than fresh juice, just-baked pastries, fresh bread and Il Mongetto's preserves, and seasonal fruit. The Monferrato area offers the same attractions as more famous Alba, with white truffles, great restaurants, cute villages, and wineries to visit, and I've been back many times.

I bump into Roberto and Margherita at food and wine fairs (they've been joined in the business by their kids, Giacomo and Ginevra), where their stand is always crowded and there's always someone they want me to meet—like Giovanni Fiore (page 61), whose cheese they pair with Il Mongetto's fantastic *Mostarda d'Uva*.

The Santopietros' original recipe calls for 70 pounds of grape must, and lengthy, slow cooking. It's much simpler to find a jar of Il Mongetto's reasonably priced *Mostarda d'Uva*. Pair mostarda with cheese, polenta, or as they once did in Piemonte, a scoop of clean, freshly fallen snow. If you'd like the recipe, though, e-mail me at info@faithwillinger.com.

MOSTLY PIEMONTESE CHEESE PLATE   DESSERT

To showcase a good *mostarda* grape chutney, serve it as part of a cheese course with soft creamy cheeses, possibly one or more of the following:

Ribiola (the best choice), either cow, sheep, goat, or mixed milk
Mascarpone
Taleggio (not from Piemonte but still a good choice)
Gorgonzola

Ernesto, Riccardo, Francesco, and Andrea Illy

ILLY MAKES my very favorite coffee. I've known the family for years: Riccardo (a progressive politician) introduced me to the rest of the family—Dottor Ernesto, the patriarch; and brothers Francesco, a dreamer who created the Francis Francis! line of espresso machines; and Andrea, who now runs the company. The company is meticulous, examining each bean with gas chromatography and rejecting any that are less than perfect, to be resold to less scrupulous roasters. The same careful attention is paid to roasting, cooling, and packing the beans.

I've tried many espresso machines, and even though it occasionally needs adjusting (not unlike a sports car), I'm in love with my current model, Illy's semi-professional Francis Francis! RS2. It uses their E.S.E. system of pods—perfectly measured and tamped portions that take all the guesswork out of espresso making. And it prepares two espresso coffees at a time, each topped with a uniform burnished tan *crema*, a sign of perfection. There's an efficient steam wand for cappuccino and the upper surface of the machine is a cup warmer, perfect for displaying my Illy espresso cup collection. (I'm crazy about the Rufus Willis espresso and cappuccino cups; they look like traditional English blue-and-white tea and coffee sets, but the scenes are of urban blight instead of idyllic countryside.)

For my Illy family friends, I've chosen the recipe for *Caffè Shakerato*, an espresso shaken over ice in a cocktail shaker. The *crema* turns into a head of foam when shaken with ice and sugar syrup—refreshing when the weather is steamy. The recipe can be doubled, but for more than two; it's best to repeat the process. Visit Illy's website to find the nearest Francis Francis! dealer in the United States or visit their caffè when you are in Trieste.

ILLY

www.illyusa.com
www.illy.com

CAFFÈ ILLY

Via delle Torri, 3
34100 Trieste
Tel/Fax: +39-040-765-251
Open 7:30 A.M.–9 P.M.,
closed Sundays.

BETWEEN MEALS

SHAKERATO ESPRESSO

SERVES 1

¼ cup sugar
2 large or 4 small ice cubes
1 freshly made espresso, preferably with Illy

Dissolve the sugar in ¼ cup water over high heat to make a sugar syrup. Cool completely.

Put the ice cubes in a metal cocktail shaker. Add ½ teaspoon (or more) of the sugar syrup, then pour the hot espresso over the cubes. Shake vigorously until the ice cubes are almost completely melted; you'll know from the sound. Strain into a stemmed martini glass.

Arrigo Cipriani

ARRIGO CIPRIANI REIGNS at Harry's Bar in Venice, sitting with his back to the wall next to the front door. We met when I directed the culinary program at the Cipriani Hotel, although it is no longer owned by his family. His idea of a restaurant, he explained, was a comfortable place with dependable cooking, where even first-time customers were treated like regulars.

Many have asked about Harry's bar and the origin of its name. The story begins with Giuseppe Cipriani, a barman at the Europa Hotel in Venice who made a strategic loan to a stranded American client. Harry Pickering eventually repaid that loan, and when he backed Giuseppe in setting up a place of his own, Guiseppe named it after his benefactor. Harry's Bar opened in 1931, in a tiny, spruced-up rope warehouse, not far from Piazza San Marco. The ambience was somewhere between a luxury hotel bar and a Venetian *bacaro* (wine bar with snacks)—understated, elegant, a place where customers felt well taken care of any time of day. He scaled down the tables, armchairs, glasses, dishes, and cutlery to the size of the room. Cipriani's wife, Giulietta, prepared a few homestyle dishes and sandwiches, but food was an afterthought and there wasn't a menu. Within a year Harry's Bar was a success, with a clientele of upper-class Venetians, nobles, and trendy European and American tourists. Giuseppe hired a chef and Giulietta retired to give birth to their first child, named Arrigo, Italian for Harry, after their backer.

Arrigo took over Harry's Bar after attending university, then rented and renovated an upstairs room that doubled the restaurant's capacity. He opened Harry's Dolci on the Giudecca, a summery, outdoors, casual, slightly less expensive version of Harry's Bar, and he transferred the pastry and pasta production to a spot nearby. But Arrigo's dream went beyond Veneto, to restaurants in New York, London, and Hong Kong.

HARRY'S BAR

Località Calle Vallaresso, 1323
San Marco
30124 Venezia
Tel: +39-041-528-5777
Fax: +39-041-520-8822
harrysbar@cipriani.com
www.cipriani.com
Always open. All credit cards accepted.

He went global with a line of first-rate products, like egg pasta as good as that served at Harry's Bar, made with pasta machines modified to his specifications. And jarred pasta sauces, rice for risotto, panettone without candied fruit (Arrigo hates it), olive oils and vinegars, coffee, and spices.

Harry's Bar is expensive, except for Venetians, who get a serious discount, but I still like to stop in for a glass of Prosecco, a Bellini or Negroni, and maybe a sandwich or chicken croquette (not on the menu but always available) or a slice of the chocolate or zabaglione cake—or just an espresso. The scene is always amusing. When I miss Harry's, I simply make their shrimp sandwiches, although I don't make the mayonnaise from scratch the way they do at Harry's, with vegetable oil—"it's lighter," Arrigo told me. Instead, I use jarred mayonnaise, whisking in a few spoonfuls of extra virgin to improve the flavor.

BETWEEN MEALS   ## SHRIMP SANDWICHES

MAKES 4 SANDWICHES

5 tablespoons mayonnaise plus a few spoonfuls of quality extra
    virgin olive oil
1 tablespoon and 1 teaspoon lemon juice
A few drops of Worcestershire sauce
¼ teaspoon dry mustard
Freshly ground white pepper
10 ounces peeled cooked shrimp (tiny shrimp or chop larger shrimp
    into small pieces)
8 thin slices good-quality sandwich bread

Whisk a few spoonfuls of extra virgin into the mayonnaise. Add the lemon juice, Worcestershire sauce, mustard, and white pepper. Reserve 2 tablespoons of the mayonnaise and combine the rest with the shrimp.

Generously spread the bread slices with the reserved mayonnaise mixture. Pile one-fourth of the shrimp mixture in a mound in the middle of a bread slice, leaving a ¾-inch margin around the edges. Top with another slice of bread, mayonnaise side down, and press the edges to seal the sandwich. Trim off the crusts. Cut in half diagonally to make two triangles with a hump in the middle. Eat with the point facing down so no shrimp fall out.

Primo and Annalisa Franco

LIKE MOST of my favorite winemakers, Primo resembles his wine —in this case a Prosecco that is lively, effervescent, and charming. When I was the director of the culinary program at the Cipriani, he was a frequent guest winemaker and he brought his wife, Annalisa, another Prosecco personality. He's held fun parties at his winery, hosting friends, winemakers, and enologists from all over Italy. We've dined together on many occasions. I was entertained by his story of *toast,* which is what the grilled-and-pressed ham and cheese sandwiches that are found in bars throughout Italy are called. It seems Primo and Annalisa were invited to a party by a group of American friends who asked Primo to make a *toast.* He thought they meant the sandwich, so he brought the ingredients to the party, assuming he'd be making a snack that would be paired with his Prosecco. Everyone was amused by his error, but loved the *toast.* Here's Primo's recipe, a version superior to that found in most Italian bars.

NINO FRANCO SPUMANTE S.R.L.
Via Garibaldi, 147
31049 Valdobbiadene (TV)
Tel: +39-0423-972-051
Fax: +39-0423-975-977
info@ninofranco.it
www.ninofranco.it
Visits by appointment only.

GRILLED HAM AND CHEESE SANDWICHES

SERVES 4 TO 6

¼ pound Italian fontina cheese
1 egg yolk
Freshly ground black pepper
12 slices white bread
¼ pound sliced ham
Extra virgin olive oil

Process or grate the fontina and mix with the egg yolkand pepper. Spread this mixture on six slices of bread. Top each with a slice of ham. Put the remaining bread slices on top of the ham.

Brush the sandwiches with the extra virgin and grill in a panino press; or add ½ teaspoon extra virgin to a nonstick skillet and sauté each sandwich, with a weight on top (like a plate), over medium heat until browned and the cheese is melted.

Slice each sandwich into four rectangles. Serve immediately.

Walter Bolzonella

BARMAN WALTER BOLZONELLA didn't invent the Bellini—that credit goes to Harry's Bar (page 83), where founder Giuseppe Cipriani created the peach and Prosecco drink in the 1930s, but Walter prepares the best version I've ever had. He presides at the bar at the Hotel Cipriani (no relation to Harry's Bar, sharing only the same founder), off the beaten track but well worth the free voyage on the hotel's private launch. The bar is comfortable, a cool place to hang out, and Walter's drinks are impeccable. His Bellini features two regional products of excellence—sparkling Prosecco wine and the white-veined-with-pink peaches known as H6, pronounced *AH-KA-SAY* although it's probably an American hybrid—which give the Bellini its rosy color. Most places use frozen peach purée and prepare the drink year-round, but Walter's is as close to traditional as they come. He makes the Bellini only in the summer, stretching the H6 season with peaches from beyond the Venetian lagoon and uses a food mill to purée the peaches. Purists should use their hands to crush the fruit through a chinois and mix the purée with a little lemon and sugar; those in a hurry can blend or process the fruit. Either way, use the best, ripest seasonal peaches you can get, even if they're not white-fleshed. And remember, this is not a sweet drink. Fill short, narrow, unstemmed glasses with your Bellini mixture. Take a sip. Close your eyes. Think Venice.

HOTEL CIPRIANI & PALAZZO VENDRAMIN

Giudecca 10
30133 Venezia
Tel: +39-041-520-7744
Fax: +39-041-520-3930
info@hotelcipriani.it
www.hotelcipriani.com
All credit cards accepted.

BETWEEN MEALS

BELLINI COCKTAIL

SERVES 6 TO 8

¾ pound ripe peaches, preferably white

3–4 raspberries (optional but probably necessary for color)

½ cup filtered water

¼ cup fresh lemon juice

2–3 teaspoons sugar

1 bottle chilled Prosecco sparkling wine

Peel and pit the peaches. Purée the peaches and raspberries in a food mill. (Walter says that a blender destroys the texture, but if you're not as traditional, a blender or processor can be used.) Combine the purée with the water, lemon juice, and sugar and refrigerate until cold.

Pour the peach purée into a pitcher and add the Prosecco. Stir gently. Pour into glasses and drink immediately.

Tuscany

Tuscany

I'VE LIVED IN FLORENCE, the capital of Tuscany, for more than thirty years and have come to be known as the Tosco-Americana. I began my Tuscan adventures when I met my future husband, Massimo, who introduced me to extra virgin olive oil, took me to *trattorie,* and taught me about foods and wines of the region. From his father I learned about wild greens, from his aunt how to make tiramisù. When Massimo and I vacationed on the Tuscan coast, in the Lucca area, we visited wineries in the Chianti and Montalcino zones, buying wine in large demijohns that we decanted into bottles, topping them off with oil, then wrapping the necks with paper to form a cap. By the late 1970s an enological revolution shook the region, with wineries interested in quality instead of selling in bulk. I got serious about wine myself, befriending a few oenologists who took me to visit the properties where they consulted. Meanwhile, an olive oil expert invited me to visit his press and sample yearly tastings, which further improved my understanding of extra virgin. I fell in love with my butcher (page 116) and so did Massimo. They've all become friends as well as invaluable sources of food knowledge, and thirty years of friends and recipes deserved a section of its own.

Andrea and Cinzia Bertucci

ITH HIS SISTER, CINZIA, Andrea Bertucci owns Il Vecchio Mulino, the most wonderful bar, which I first wrote about in *Eating in Italy*. The village of Castelnuovo Garfagnana is in a part of Tuscany that most visitors don't get to, although the train that runs north from Lucca makes the trip easy enough. It's worth the journey to meet Andrea and for the chance to shop for the extraordinary variety of products from the Garfagnana area. You'll find beans, farro (a barley-like grain), stone-ground heirloom cornmeal, and chestnut flour, all organic. After all, who could afford or even procure chemical fertilizers in the impoverished, isolated mountains?

Il Vecchio Mulino is a bar where locals stop in for a coffee, snack, or glass of wine, and to hang out at the counter, at tables, or on the bench outside the bar. Local reds, important Italian wines, and even French wines are sold by the glass. Andrea knows everyone in town and beyond, and supplies many restaurants with the products he's so proud to serve at his bar. He's a great source of intelligence on the Garfagnana area and its traditions. For instance, Andrea filled me in on Garfagnana chestnut lore; he's got an adorable way of pronouncing *chestnuts* in English—it sounds like "cheese-nuts." Wheat didn't grow in the area, so locals used chestnut flour to make bread, polenta, and simple desserts. Chestnut polenta is served here as an appetizer, flavored with rosemary and paired with pork, or for dessert with a few spoonfuls of ricotta and grated bittersweet chocolate. Andrea's sister, Cinzia, offers her chestnut polenta "bites" as a favorite bar snack at Il Vecchio Mulino; she prepares them in advance and Andrea heats them up at the bar. Paired with a big red wine, they're perfect for a wonderful midafternoon snack.

IL VECCHIO MULINO

Via Vittorio Emanuele, 12
55032 Castelnuovo
Garfagnana (LU)
Tel: +39-0583-621-92
Fax: +39-0583-626-16
info@ilvecchiomulino.com
www.ilvecchiomulino.com
Open 7:30 A.M.–8 P.M.
Monday–Saturday; closed
Sundays.

GARFAGNANA DOP CHESTNUT POLENTA "BITES" WITH PANCETTA

SERVES 6 TO 8

2½ cups chestnut flour

3–3½ cups filtered water

1 teaspoon extra virgin olive oil

1 tablespoon minced fresh rosemary

1 tablespoon minced fresh sage

1 tablespoon minced fresh flat-leaf parsley

1 teaspoon fennel pollen, or ½ teaspoon chopped fennel seed

4–6 ounces pancetta, thinly sliced, or quality bacon

In a 3-quart, heavy-bottomed or nonstick pot, whisk the chestnut flour and 3 cups filtered water to combine well and eliminate all lumps. Bring the polenta to a simmer and cook, stirring with a wooden spoon, for 30 to 45 minutes. Add more filtered water, a tablespoon or two at a time, if the polenta gets too thick. Cool the chestnut polenta until just warm.

Measure a piece of parchment paper to amply fit a jellyroll pan. Oil the paper with the extra virgin and place it in the pan, oil side up.

Stir the rosemary, sage, parsley, and fennel into the polenta. Spread the polenta on a separate piece of oiled parchment and let cool. Put the polenta into a pastry bag and, with the widest tip, pipe heaping tablespoonfuls onto a clean cutting board. (Or scoop heaping tablespoonfuls of polenta onto the cutting board.)

Preheat the oven to 375°F.

Wrap each chestnut polenta ball with half of a pancetta or bacon strip. Place in the jellyroll pan and bake for 18 to 22 minutes. Serve hot.

*   *   *

Valeria Piccini and Maurizio Menichetti

THIS RECIPE comes from a special dinner Valeria cooked to benefit tsunami victims, but I've known her and her sommelier/host husband, Maurizio Menichetti, since I researched the first edition of *Eating in Italy* in the mid-'80s. Their restaurant Da Caino is in the southern part of Tuscany, in the medieval village of Montemerano, and it features an inn with three beautiful rooms upstairs so diners can spend the night, use the village as a base for touring the area, and devote serious attention to Maurizio's spectacular wine list. They've also opened an enoteca where wines and homemade products like cookies, preserves, jarred vegetables, sauces for pasta, and more can be purchased.

DA CAINO
Via Canonica, 3
58050 Montemerano (GR)
Tel: +39-0564-602-817
Fax: +39-0564-602-807
info@dacaino.it
www.dacaino.it
Closed all day Wednesday and Thursday at lunch.

SWEET AND SOUR CHICKEN BITES

SERVES 4 TO 6

4 boneless chicken thighs
1 garlic clove
1 teaspoon fresh sage leaves
1 teaspoon fresh rosemary leaves
½ teaspoon fine sea salt
Freshly ground black pepper
2 tablespoons mild honey
¼ cup white wine vinegar
2 tablespoons extra virgin olive oil
2 tablespoons dry white wine

Cut the chicken thighs into bite-size pieces. Mince the garlic, sage, and rosemary together and combine with the salt and pepper. Mix the chicken pieces with the herb mixture, cover, and marinate in the refrigerator for 2 hours or more.

Combine the honey and vinegar in a small saucepan and melt over low heat, stirring to combine. (You can also heat them in a microwave and stir to combine.) Set aside.

Heat the extra virgin in a medium nonstick skillet, add the chicken pieces, and sauté over high heat to brown lightly. Add the white wine and when it's evaporated, add the vinegar-honey mixture. Cook over highest heat to evaporate the liquid, until the sauce is shiny and coats the chicken pieces. Season with additional salt and pepper, if necessary. Serve with toothpicks as an appetizer.

* * *

Guido and Giulia Pinzani

GUIDO PINZANI and his attractive daughter Giulia, cheesemakers from Tuscany, own a high-tech, super-hygienic dairy where the raw milk from 20,000 sheep that graze in the areas of Siena and Volterra is transformed into traditional and New Wave cheeses. Most pecorino is made from pasteurized milk, and less than scrupulous producers even mix cows' and sheep's milk. At Guido's *caseificio,* the milk is heated to only 95°F., conserving the natural bacteria that help turn milk into cheese and confer the complex flavors that are added artificially by those who use pasteurized milk. We tasted, beginning with the most delicate cheese—ricotta—just-made, still warm. Marzolino, eaten after only a month of aging, is made in the spring (the name derives from *Marzo* [March], when it was traditionally made). Classico, as its name declares, is a classic pecorino. Classico Riserva is aged more than twelve months. Rugoso (named for its wrinkled rind) is a naturally refermented cheese that is aged for almost a year. San Gimignano is a saffron-flavored pecorino, and there are two versions of pecorino flavored with black and white truffles. The innovative Blu, a sheep's milk cheese veined with selected molds, is a complex blue cheese that's bound to become a new tradition.

CASEIFICIO CAVALIER EMILIO PINZANI

Località Castel San Gimignano
53034 Colle Val D'Elsa (SI)
Tel: +39-0577-953-005
Visits by appointment only.

I left the Pinzani dairy with huge hunks of cheese and a basket of just-made ricotta. I piped the ricotta into zucchini flowers and simply heated them in a skillet with a little extra virgin. My guests were wild about the dish, which showcased the amazingly high quality of the ricotta, as well as the fresh flavors of the zucchini flowers, which are usually masked with batter and deep-fried. I served them to Guido and Giulia when they came to dinner, toting fresh ricotta, and it met with their enthusiastic approval. Home-gardeners should pick male zucchini flowers (the ones on the longer stems, not those eventually attached to zucchini, which are the females) in the morning or evening when they're tightly closed.

RICOTTA-STUFFED ZUCCHINI FLOWERS

SERVES 4 TO 6

1 cup ricotta, fresh if possible, or sheep's milk ricotta
12–16 fresh zucchini flowers
3 tablespoons extra virgin olive oil
Freshly ground black pepper
Fine sea salt
1 tablespoon minced fresh basil

If your ricotta is watery, drain it in a sieve to remove excess whey. Soak the zucchini flowers in cool water, then spin-dry in a salad spinner. Removing the stamens is unnecessary.

Pack the ricotta into a pastry bag—I use a disposable one and simply cut the tip off the end. Insert the end of the pastry bag into the zucchini flowers and pipe one or two spoonfuls of ricotta into each.

Drizzle 1 tablespoon extra virgin in a large nonstick skillet. Place the stuffed flowers in the skillet in a single layer and place the pan over the highest heat. When the pan heats and the oil begins to sizzle, cover and cook for 4 to 6 minutes or until the flowers are hot, steamed by the moisture of the ricotta. Transfer to a serving dish and top with pepper, sea salt, minced basil, and the remaining extra virgin.

Armando Manni

RMANDO MANNI makes Italy's most expensive extra virgin olive
oils. When Armando's son Lorenzo was born, he felt that his child
should eat only the most perfect, healthy, wonderful foods. Armando
spoke to some doctors who told him that extra virgin olive oil, at its very
best, had many beneficial effects. He worked with doctors and researchers
who analyzed his extra virgin, and they found it extremely high in
polyphenols—important antioxidants that are anti-bad-cholesterol, anti-
heart-attack, anti-cancer, and anti-aging agents. He decided to make two
oils, the first for his son, which he called *Per mio figlio,* with delicate flavors that would appeal to a baby because it was made from riper olives
instead of the usual blend of ripe and green olives. Since he liked the
zesty traditional taste of extra virgin, he made a second oil for himself,
Per me, with less-ripe olives grown on the upper slopes of Monte Amiata,
the highest elevation where olive trees can survive. He packaged the oil
in slender 100 ml (3.4-ounce) bottles made of anti-UVA glass, since light
causes olive oil to oxidize. He bottled the oil under inert gas and used a
special plastic cork to maintain freshness, also preserving all the healthful
properties of just-pressed oil, which normally diminish over time. Both
oils are sold together in an attractive tan cardboard box tied closed with a
Per me–Per mio figlio brown and black ribbon.

Armando's extra virgins are perfect, balanced—*Per me* with spicy,
complex flavors and *Per mio figlio* delicate, silky—both best used as a
condiment. I like to open both bottles for friends and have plenty of
bread and simply prepared vegetables, like beans, boiled cauliflower, and
baked potatoes, all perfect for tasting the difference between *Per me* and
Per mio figlio.

Armando's recipe for Spaghetti with Parmigiano-Reggiano and Extra
Virgin is clearly something he makes all the time, and it can be scaled

OLIO MANNI

Monte Amiata
58038 Seggiano (GR)
Tel/Fax: +39-06-591-5880
Cell: +39-329-404-0099
info@manni.biz
www.manni.biz
Visits by appointment only.

down for one serving or increased to a maximum of six, after which it becomes too difficult to manage. It's made with simple, healthy, impeccable ingredients that are always on hand in Armando's kitchen and should be in yours: a chunk of aged Parmigiano-Reggiano—when it's aged 24 months it's the most digestible of cheeses (recommended by the same doctors who analyzed his oils), even for the lactose intolerant—and *Per me,* the zestier oil; if you can't find Armando's oil, use the very best, freshest extra virgin you can find. Most quality oils have the harvest date, which should be from the most recent November or December. Check out Armando's impressive website, www.manni.biz, to find out more about the healthful benefits of his extra virgins or to purchase his oils.

FIRST COURSE

SPAGHETTI WITH PARMIGIANO-REGGIANO AND ARMANDO'S EXTRA VIRGIN

SERVES 2

Sea salt
7 ounces spaghetti or spaghettini
3 tablespoons *Per me* or other fine, fresh extra virgin olive oil
Freshly ground black pepper
1 cup freshly grated aged Parmigiano-Reggiano cheese

Bring 5 or 6 quarts of water to a rolling boil; add 3 tablespoons salt and the pasta. Stir occasionally with a wooden fork or spoon. Cook until almost al dente.

Meanwhile, put the extra virgin and the pepper into a large skillet. When the pasta is almost cooked, measure ½ cup of the pasta-cooking water into the skillet, and place over medium heat.

When the pasta is al dente, drain it, reserving 1 cup of the pasta water and add the pasta to the skillet. Stir the pasta and the liquid in the skillet, add ¾ cup cheese, and stir over high heat with a wooden fork until a creamy sauce is formed and the pasta is cooked. (Armando says not to place the skillet on the heat, but to hold it above the heat. I find this maneuver difficult, but offer it as an option for those who want to follow Armando's recipe to the letter.) Add the reserved pasta-cooking water if sauce is too dry. Serve with remaining Parmigiano-Reggiano.

Fulvio and Emanuela Pierangelini

FULVIO PIERANGELINI and his wife, Emanuela, own the restaurant Gambero Rosso (named for the osteria in Pinocchio) on the coast of Tuscany. It's considered one of Italy's best restaurants. I was taken there for lunch by the owners of a nearby winery, and I was very impressed. The restaurant overlooks the harbor of San Vincenzo, and the sea inspires many of Fulvio's dishes. Pristinely fresh local seafood is treated with respect; tastes are simple, refined, dressed with superior extra virgin. Pork is from the cinta Senese breed. The wine list is excellent, personal, especially strong and deep on local super-Tuscans. Emanuela runs the dining room with style and the service is professional, the crystal, china, silver, and linens all first-class. *Passatina di ceci*, a creamy chickpea soup topped with shrimp, Fulvio's signature, has become a new classic, found in restaurants throughout Italy. It was a dish he created for cousins Marchese Incisa della Rocchetta, owner of Sassicaia, and Marchese Lodovico Antinori, owner of Ornellaia (both considered producers of some of Italy's finest wines), who planned to have lunch at the restaurant and discuss business. It was closed, but Fulvio had stopped off to pick up some papers on the way home. He offered to make lunch at home for the illustrious winery owners, thinking they'd decline, and when they didn't, he had to scramble to find something to serve them. He had some fantastic shrimp, but not enough for a main

GAMBERO ROSSO
Piazza della Vittoria, 13
57027 San Vincenzo (LI)
Tel: +39-0565-701-021
Fax: +39-0565-704-542
Closed Monday and Tuesday;
closed October 29–January 12.
All credit cards accepted.

course, as well as some cooked chickpeas, so he created a chickpea soup, topped with steamed shrimp, and garnished it with superb extra virgin. It was an instant success, although the deal between della Rocchetta and Antinori wasn't concluded.

CHICKPEA PURÉE WITH SHRIMP

SERVES 4

1 cup dried chickpeas
Sea salt and freshly ground black pepper
1 garlic clove
1 sprig fresh rosemary
16–20 ounces fresh shrimp, in shells
3–4 tablespoons extra virgin olive oil

Put the chickpeas in a large pot, cover with about an inch of water, mix in 3 tablespoons sea salt, and soak for at least 12 hours.

Drain the chickpeas, rinse them, and put them in a 3-quart pot. Cover with water by about 3 inches, then add the garlic and rosemary. Over low heat, bring the water to a boil and simmer at least 1 hour, until the chickpeas are tender. Add ½ cup boiling water if the liquid gets too low.

Purée the chickpeas with your method of choice. (Fulvio purées his through a sieve, but the fine disk of a food mill works well, too. Puréeing with a processor or immersion mixer grinds up the skins and produces a less refined soup.) Thin the soup to desired consistency (a little thicker than heavy cream is ideal) with some of the chickpea broth; add boiling water if there's not enough broth. Season with salt and pepper, and keep warm.

Remove the shells and black veins from the shrimp. Put them in a steamer basket over ½ cup boiling water in a pot, cover, and steam for 2 to 3 minutes, until they turn pink.

Put one-fourth of the chickpea purée in each soup bowl, top each with 4 or 5 shrimp, then add a drizzle of extra virgin and freshly ground black pepper. Serve.

Maurizio Castelli

As a consulting winemaker, Maurizio Castelli is responsible for some of my favorite wines, like Grattamacco and Argiano in Montalcino, but he is also handsome and fun, and interested in music, old cars, and the world beyond the wine glass. Maurizio is a frequent guest in my kitchen for dinner, a guy with a discriminating palate and a hearty appetite—and he always brings a few bottles of wine and extra virgin, sometimes from his client McEvoy, in California. I let him choose some of the wines for dinner from a big demijohn basket next to my kitchen door; the top layer is stuff I think he'll be interested in.

MAURIZIO CASTELLI

Via del Castello, 42
53020 Montisi San Giovanni d'Asso (SI)
Tel: +39-0577-845-142
Cell: +39-335-548-7688
mcastelli@si.nettuno.it
www.mcevoyranch.com

His passion for olive oil is almost as great as his passion for wine, and while working for Castello di Volpaia he ordered a sinolea mill for extra virgin production, New Wave technology that doesn't press the oil out of the olives, but rather extracts it with a far gentler method of blades thrust into the olive pulp, removed, and scraped of clinging oil. While writing a piece on extra virgin olive oil, I took a photographer to see the sinolea production at Volpaia. After Maurizio showed us around and explained the process, he drove us to his nearby home and made lunch, using extra virgins with abandon. He's a world-class cook, and his small but perfect kitchen has a wood-burning hearth for grilling, a stove, and copper pots that he actually uses. I sat at the kitchen table while he cooked and asked him about extra virgin, the recipes, and his style of cooking. He sautéed the soffritto for his soup with extra virgin in a copper pot, commenting while adding ingredients: "I like the gentle heat of copper . . . I always cook with great extra virgin—why bother with anything else? It's my mother's recipe." While the soup simmered he cleaned and trimmed fennel, carrots, and celery for an appetizer of *pinzimonio,* or raw vegetables served with a little bowl of extra virgin (just pressed, straight from the mill) and salt. Maurizio tended the fire in the hearth, we drank Chianti, and we listened to some South American jazz while the soup cooled. He grilled a Florentine T-bone steak, and served it with a drizzle of his just-pressed oil. And I got the recipe for his mother's lentil soup.

LENTIL SOUP

SERVES 4 TO 6

¼ cup best-quality Tuscan extra virgin olive oil, plus more
    to garnish
1 carrot, peeled and minced
1 red onion, minced
1 leek, cleaned, trimmed, and minced
1 celery rib, minced
2 garlic cloves, minced
1 cup lentils, rinsed
Coarse sea salt and freshly ground black pepper

Heat the oil in a heavy-bottomed pot. Sauté the carrot, onion, most of the minced leek (save a little leek for the garnish), celery, and garlic over high heat until they begin to brown. Add the lentils, 5 cups of water, and 1 teaspoon sea salt. Bring to a boil over high heat, lower the heat, and simmer for 45 minutes, stirring occasionally, until the lentils are cooked. Skim off any gray scum that rises to the surface, and add an extra cup of water if the soup dries too much. Taste for salt, adding more if necessary, and season with pepper. Turn off the heat and let the soup rest for 20 minutes.

Ladle the warm soup into bowls and garnish with a drizzle of extra virgin and the reserved minced leek.

*   *   *

Paolo Fanciulli

PAOLO FANCIULLI

58010 Talamone Fontablanda (GR)

Tel: +39-0564-88-4921

or +39-333-284-6199

Price: about 80 euros per person, no credit cards accepted.

THE INVENTOR of *pescaturismo*—ecological fisherman meets tourist, with lunch—answers his cell phone "Paolo, *il pescatore*" (Paolo, the fisherman) and gives an invitation to head for the Tuscan coast for a day of fishing. Strawberry-blond, blue-eyed, and buff, Paolo Fanciulli is an official park guide, an environmental activist, and a member of Greenpeace; his boat *Sirene* flies a WWF (World Wildlife Fund) flag. He takes visitors along the coast of the Maremma Park, departing from the port of Talamone, south of Grosseto.

Passengers meet at the port at 8 A.M., stow their bags and backpacks in *Sirene*'s cabin, and find a place on board in the sun or shade as Paolo navigates along the coast, cruising over sea-grass meadows that have been partially destroyed by illegal drag-net fishing. The sea grass provides nutrients, releases oxygen, and prevents erosion; without it, the fish population diminishes. By fishing with tourists, Paolo and his assistant set out just one-quarter of the nets they'd need if they had to sell the catch. Not only do they increase everyone's awareness of the environmental problems and the effort it takes to get fish to the table but they also leave more fish for another day.

Paolo flings a round cast-net into the sea and harvests a few squirming handfuls of *rossetti,* or goby, a tiny see-through boneless fish bound for a future pasta sauce. I replicated his recipe at home with tiny strips of sole, not quite the same but a readily available substitute for the *rossetti.* Visitors to the coast of Tuscany can contact Paolo, spend the day on the *Sirene,* and taste the real thing.

SERVES 6

4 cups filtered water

2 teaspoons fine sea salt

6–8 ounces fish fillets

2–3 tablespoons coarse sea salt

12 ounces short pasta, like penne

1 small white onion, chopped

2 garlic cloves, peeled

¼ cup Tuscan extra virgin olive oil

Fine sea salt and freshly ground black pepper

3 tablespoons white wine

½ teaspoon grated lemon zest

2 teaspoons minced fresh flat-leaf parsley

To make the seawater (since most of us don't cook on a boat), dissolve the fine sea salt in the water in a shallow pan. In a large pot, bring 6 to 8 quarts of water to a boil.

Slice the fish fillets into thin strips and rinse the strips in the seawater. Add 2 to 3 tablespoons sea salt to the boiling water and then add the pasta.

While the pasta is cooking, place the onion and garlic in a 4-quart pot, drizzle with 2 tablespoons of the extra virgin, and cook over low heat until the onion is transparent, about 3 minutes. Add the fish strips, season with salt and pepper, and stir; add the wine and cook over highest heat to evaporate the liquid. Remove the garlic, then add the lemon zest and parsley.

Drain the pasta, reserving ½ cup of the pasta-cooking water. Add the pasta to the sauce and cook over high heat for a minute or two, adding some of the pasta-cooking water. Drizzle with the remaining 2 tablespoons extra virgin, stir to combine, and serve.

Torquato Innocenti

MY MUSE Torquato Innocenti was the inspiration for my book about Italian vegetables, *Red, White & Greens*. Customers grew impatient at his stand in the Santo Spirito market as he recounted recipes while he weighed, calculated the price, and wrapped his pre-organic (never asked for certification) produce, and I took notes. The recipes were simple and always began with a "puddle" of oil—extra virgin, of course. Torquato died a few years ago, and his sons Valerio and Antonio (page 148) continue to sell their vegetables at the market, although their discussions concern the environment, changing weather, and its effect on their produce rather than recipes.

In addition to produce, Torquato sold a small selection of other farm-fresh products. His eggs, highly sought after, were sold by the pair, only for the first customers of the day; rabbits were available by special order and came whole, skinned, gutted, and wrapped in news-paper. Torquato told me not to throw away the head because it made a great sauce for pasta, and though he was right, I knew I couldn't publish a recipe in which the first step directs the cook to "gouge out the eyeballs." So I tried making the sauce with chicken backs, with most favorable results. I miss Torquato, but think of him often whenever I buy Innocenti produce and prepare his recipes.

FUSILLI WITH CHICKEN BONE SAUCE

SERVES 4 TO 6

2 large chicken backs or a leftover chicken carcass

¼ cup extra virgin olive oil

1 carrot, chopped

1 celery stalk, chopped

1 onion, chopped

2 garlic cloves, chopped

1 teaspoon chopped fresh rosemary leaves

½ teaspoon chopped fresh sage

¼ teaspoon fennel pollen or fennel seeds

Chili pepper to taste

2 cups dry red wine (optional)

Sea salt

14–16 ounces fusilli or other short pasta

½ cup grated Parmigiano-Reggiano cheese

Cut each chicken back into two or three pieces, or cut the chicken carcass into manageable pieces. Heat 1 tablespoon of the extra virgin over high heat in a 4-quart heavy-bottomed pot. Sauté the chicken until browned. Remove from the pot, add the remaining extra virgin, lower the heat, and sauté the carrot, celery, onion, garlic, rosemary, sage, fennel pollen or seeds, and chili pepper and cook for 5 minutes, until the vegetables soften. Add the browned chicken, turn the heat to high, and add the wine and 2 cups of water (or simply 4 cups of water) to cover the chicken by around 2 inches. When the liquid begins to simmer, lower the heat, and cook for 2 hours, until the meat falls off the bones.

Remove the chicken pieces and cool. Skim the excess fat from the sauce. Pick the chicken meat off the bones and chop coarsely. Add to the pot and season with salt.

Bring a large pot with 5 quarts of water to a rolling boil; add 3 table-

(recipe continues)

spoons sea salt and the pasta. Cook the pasta until it offers considerable resistance to the tooth—around three-quarters of the recommended package cooking time. Drain the pasta, reserving a cup of the pasta-cooking water.

Add the pasta to the sauce and cook over high heat to amalgamate. Add some of the pasta-cooking water if sauce dries out too much before pasta is cooked. Serve the pasta topped with grated cheese.

Fabio Picchi and Maria Cassi

ABIO PICCHI OWNS my favorite restaurant in Florence, Cibrèo, next to the Sant'Ambrogio market. We've been friends for a long time, have dined and traveled together, and I was his witness at his marriage to comedian Maria Cassi. His style, culinary and non, is unique, and he's created a gastronomic empire, with a bar, restaurant, trattoria, and his latest, most genial idea, a private club/theater.

A shop in the club's entrance sells interesting products like great canned tuna, preserves and preserved vegetables made by the restaurant, and most important, a full line of Sicilian sea salts. When I handed him a box of salt I'd brought back from a trip to Sicilian saltpans, Fabio was skeptical—"salt is salt," he told me—but after a taste he became a believer. Now he considers salt such a basic component of a meal that he named his club Teatro del Sale (salt theater). Club members dine at two large tables, one in front of the open kitchen, or at tables built around columns and along the walls. A large table is covered with platters of salads, vegetables, cold dishes, stacks of plates, baskets of bread, and cutlery, while another holds red and white wine and other beverages, which are included in the price of the meals. Fabio theatrically calls out the names of the hot dishes as they're passed from the kitchen to the buffet. Breakfast, lunch, and dinner are served buffet-style.

Dinner service stops at 9:30, when there's a stage show, which could be live music, comedy, or poetry reading (the schedule is posted on their website). Fabio's wife, Maria, performs occasionally, and her evenings sell out quickly.

When Fabio makes this recipe he uses anchovies that are caught by lamplight and filleted by his fishmonger, but he said the recipe works with any full-flavored fresh fish, such as anchovies, bluefish, or mackerel. He also suggested thinly sliced swordfish, halibut, or tuna as a substitute.

CIBRÈO CITTÀ APERTA RISTORANTE, TRATTORIA, CAFFÈ, TEATRO, NEGOZIO

Via A. del Verrocchio, 8r;

Via dei Macci, 122r

50122 Firenze

Tel: +39-055-234-1100

Fax: +39-055-244-966

cibreo.fi@tin.it

www.cibreo.com

Closed Sundays and Mondays.

BREADCRUMBED BAKED FISH AND POTATO TORTINO

SERVES 4 TO 6

1½ pounds potatoes

2 garlic cloves, minced

2 tablespoons chopped fresh parsley

Sea salt and freshly ground black pepper

1 dried chili pepper, minced (Fabio's pepperoncini chili peppers are
   grown by his father, dried, then finely ground)

½–1 cup extra virgin olive oil

2 heaping teaspoons dried (but not old) oregano

1 tablespoon lemon zest

1 teaspoon fennel seeds

½ cup tomato pulp (peeled and seeded fresh or canned tomatoes)

2 pounds fresh full-flavored fish fillets (anchovies, sardines, bluefish,
   or mackerel), or 1 pound swordfish, halibut, or tuna steaks,
   sliced ¼-inch thick

2 tablespoons chopped fresh basil

⅓ cup unflavored bread crumbs

Boil the potatoes, cool until manageable, and cut into bite-size pieces. Dress them with the garlic, 1 tablespoon of parsley, salt, pepper, some of the chili pepper, and ¼ to ½ cup of the extra virgin and stir to combine. Put the potatoes in an 8 by 10-inch baking dish in one layer.

Mince 1 heaping teaspoon of the oregano with the lemon zest and fennel seeds. Sprinkle over the potatoes and scatter half the tomato pulp over the potatoes. Place a layer of fish (skin side up if you're using filleted fish) over the potatoes to completely cover. Season with salt, pepper, the remaining chili pepper, oregano, parsley, and the basil and scatter with the remaining tomato pulp. Top with the bread crumbs and drizzle with extra virgin. Refrigerate for 1 hour.

Preheat the oven to 550°F.

Bake for 10 to 15 minutes, depending on the thickness of the fish, until the bread crumbs are browned and the fish is cooked through. Serve hot or at room temperature.

Bettina Rogosky

BETTINA ROGOSKY makes one of Italy's greatest wines, Caberlot, a varietal that's a hybrid of cabernet and merlot (not a blend) at her farm, Il Carnasciale, south of Florence. I was invited to meet her and taste her wine at Cibrèo (page 109)—Bettina's favorite restaurant (mine, too) in Florence—at a wine-tasting lunch. There were magnums of Tuscany's greatest cabernet blends, legendary, unaffordable, to compare with Caberlot. I thought I'd be polite, taste her wine, then suck up all the good stuff. The Caberlot knocked my socks off, the best wine on the table: elegant, rounded tannins, beautiful finish, Tuscan but not really, just like its producer. Bettina was charming, stunning, had lived in New York, resided in Paris, stayed at the farm whenever she could get away, loved to cook. Of course we became friends.

PODERE IL CARNASCIALE
52020 Mercatale Valdarno (AR)
Tel: +39-055-991-1142
Fax: +39-055-992-957
Visits by appointment only.

I visited the farm during the grape harvest, helped destem the grapes by hand, stomp on them in a wooden barrel; the production was so small that they pressed grapes with a low-tech, old-fashioned method—by foot. All this hard work was followed, after a foot rinse, by lunch. The farmhouse has been restored with spectacular taste: huge wooden beams, high ceilings, white walls, terra-cotta floors, comfortable sofas, interesting art, objects, books, and a fire burning in the hearth. Bettina's farm produces superior extra virgin olive oil, packaged in an attractive clay bottle—it sat in the center of the table. She wasn't planning to serve her wine at lunch. "We don't really have enough, only 1,000 magnums, and I like to taste other wines," she told me. I begged. And her Caberlot was a fantastic match with the roasted lamb shoulder, a tiny animal, each shoulder weighing less than 2 pounds, half the size of lamb found in the United States. If you can get tiny lamb, use shoulder for this recipe, otherwise substitute lamb shanks.

MAIN COURSE

ROAST LAMB SHOULDER WITH ROOT VEGETABLES

SERVES 4 TO 6

1 pound small potatoes
½ pound carrots
½ pound turnips and/or parsnips
4 ounces scallions
4 lamb shanks, around 1 pound or less apiece, or
    2 1½–1¾ pound lamb shoulder pieces, with bones
Fine sea salt and freshly ground black pepper
4 tablespoons extra virgin olive oil
¼ cup butter or additional extra virgin olive oil
½ teaspoon sugar
10 garlic cloves, unpeeled
6–8 sprigs fresh thyme
1–2 tablespoons minced flat-leaf parsley

Preheat the oven to 400°F.

Peel the potatoes, carrots, and turnips and/or parsnips and cut into bite-size pieces. Remove the root ends and outer layer of the scallions and trim off the toughest part of the stem ends.

Season the meat with salt and pepper.

In a large skillet, heat 2 tablespoons extra virgin and brown the meat on all sides.

Melt the butter (or extra virgin) in a 6-quart, flameproof, heavy-bottomed casserole. Add the potatoes, carrots, turnips, and scallions; mix to combine with the oil and/or butter, season with salt, pepper, and sugar, and sauté to heat the vegetables. Add the garlic and thyme. Put the meat on top of the vegetables and bake for 1 hour.

After 30 minutes, add about ¼ cup boiling water and stir the vegetables. Cook for another 30 minutes. Lower the heat to 300°F., add another ¼ cup boiling water if necessary, stir the vegetables, and cook for another 30 minutes. The meat will be tender and come easily off the bone. Cut the meat into pieces—neatness doesn't count—and place on the root vegetables. Sprinkle with parsley and serve.

Stefano Campatelli, Marta Ripaccioli, and the Brunello Consortium

I'VE BEEN friendly with the people from the Brunello di Montalcino wine consortium for a long time, ever since they elected me to an international jury for their annual Leccio d'Oro awards. It didn't take me long to accept—the other jury members were cool and I'm crazy about Brunello di Montalcino, one of Italy's greatest wines, as well as Rosso di Montalcino, which is younger, less expensive, less important. My job would require drinking Brunello at meetings and discussing possible candidates for three awards: restaurant, trattoria or casual dining, and wine-shop/enoteca, all with especially strong Italian wine lists, with special attention to Brunello di Montalcino. I would have to show up in February for their event, Benvenuto Brunello, to welcome the latest vintages with a tasting of both Brunello and Rosso di Montalcino from most of the 240 consortium members.

Stefano Campatelli is the head of the consortium. He calls to arrange the meetings, often at places that have won the prizes in the past, like Hostaria da Ivan (page 52) or Cibrèo (page 109), or in Milan, since that's where many of the other jury members are from. Marta Ripaccioli organizes the Benvenuto Brunello event, assigns rooms at Montalcino hotels, and gives out seating assignments for dinner at Castello Banfi. I get preferential treatment since I have to present the awards on the stage of Montalcino's "Little Theater." For all this hard work, I get a case of Brunello di Montalcino and a case of Rosso di Montalcino. This is definitely my kind of jury duty.

Marta gave me her recipe for Scottiglia, a traditional braised meat dish—her version is with chicken, but rabbit or lamb can also be used. Of course the wine used in the recipe is Brunello di Montalcino, but it's only ½ cup and you'll have the rest of the bottle to drink with your meal.

CONSORZIO DEL VINO BRUNELLO DI MONTALCINO

Costa del Municipio, 1
53024 Montalcino (SI)
Tel: +39-0577-849-246
Fax: +39-0577-849-425
info@consorziobrunellodi
montalcino.it
www.consorziobrunellodi
montalcino.it
Visits by appointment only.

MONTALCINO STEWED CHICKEN

SERVES 4

4 garlic cloves

1 medium onion

2 tablespoons fresh rosemary leaves

2 tablespoons flat-leaf parsley leaves

1 celery rib

1 chicken, around 3 pounds, cut into 6–10 serving pieces

Sea salt and freshly ground black pepper

½ cup Brunello di Montalcino (or Rosso di Montalcino, for a less
   expensive option)

2 cups puréed canned plum tomatoes

1 fresh chili pepper or dried red pepper flakes to taste

Mince the garlic, onion, rosemary, parsley, and celery.

Put the chicken pieces in a 4-quart, heavy-bottomed pot and place over medium heat. Sauté until lightly browned, season with salt and pepper, and remove excess fat. Add the minced herb mixture, stir to combine, and cook for a few minutes.

Add the wine, raise the heat to high, and evaporate the wine. Add the tomato purée, season with salt, pepper, and chili pepper. When the sauce comes to a simmer, lower the heat and cook for 20 to 25 minutes, uncovered, or until chicken is done. If the sauce appears too dry, add a little water. Serve.

*   *   *

Dario Cecchini

ANTICA MACELLERIA CECCHINI

Via XX Luglio, 11

50022 Panzano in Chianti (FI)

Tel: +39-055-852-020

Open from 8 A.M.–2 P.M. Closed on Wednesdays.

DARIO CECCHINI is the most famous butcher in Italy and therefore deserves two recipes in this book. He calls me his American sister, and I'm thrilled to have such an illustrious Tuscan brother. His shop in the village of Panzano in Chianti draws visitors from all over the world, who come to taste *salumi,* sample a glass of wine, and purchase some of Dario's flavored salt, Profumo del Chianti. When I visited the salt pans of Trapani and returned with some of the Sicilian salt for Dario, he paired it with the herbs of his area—rosemary, thyme, sage, fennel pollen, lavender, and more—and now sells it at the shop in jars or Cryovak packs.

Dario sells the best steaks I've ever had, both the classic Fiorentina T-bone steak and the Panzanese, named for his hometown and cut from the heart of the rump. It's a monumental slab of meat, personally selected by Dario and thick enough to stand up. According to Dario, the cut dates from before the Renaissance, when it was known as the *tagliata.* I grill his steaks in my kitchen hearth, but I'm not as fussy as Dario about the kind of wood I use. I'm not sure what he'd think of a gas grill and don't want to ask, but I *do* know he'd hate a broiler. In a break with tradition, Dario never salts his meat before grilling, and forget about sauce—salt, pepper (or Profumo del Chianti), and a drizzle of extra virgin are the only condiments Dario approves of; and true food lovers, he says, will eat the Panzanese without any additions at all. Dario's instructions to those who purchase his steak caution: "Bear in mind: A well-prepared connoisseur could have the following side effects—extreme sensations, profound physical enjoyment, stimulation to drink 'big' red wine, an awakening of the affectionate senses (with all that follows)." I doubt if most supermarket meat will produce the same results.

According to Dario, the Panzanese isn't meat, it's an emotion—one of life's joys. Readers should purchase the best, thickest steak they can and follow as many of Dario's "commandments" as they can. Don't use metal implements to turn meat—only wooden tongs or, if you want to imitate Dario, your hands. Accompany it with an ample supply of Chianti Classico, of course. Order by mail if you haven't got a butcher or quality meat shop nearby.

When I was testing recipes for *Red, White & Greens,* I brought Dario a taste of Tuna Rabbit, which I'd made with chicken—poached, then marinated under oil, just like tuna. It reminded Dario of a recipe for pork that a butcher had once mentioned to him. And so Tonno del Chianti was born. It was an instant success in Panzano and beyond. The pork, just like tuna, is poached in water, not oil like confit, although the texture of the meat (or fish) is similar. Serve just like tuna—in Tuscany, this means paired with beans. Use the olive oil as a dressing for the beans.

LA PANZANESE GRILLED STEAK

SERVES 4 TO 6

2½–3-inch-thick steak (2–3 pounds), such as sirloin, porterhouse,
  or T-bone
1 tablespoon extra virgin olive oil (optional)
Fine sea salt (if you haven't got any Profumo del Chianti)
Freshly ground black pepper

Remove the steak from the refrigerator 8 to 10 hours before cooking.
Prepare the grill, filled with red-hot coals of "noble" hard wood if
possible.

Cook the steak for 5 minutes on each side, then stand the steak on
end and cook for 15 minutes standing up, rotating the steak on its side
every 5 minutes. Those who prefer their meat medium-rare can cook for
a few minutes more—I won't tell Dario.

Let the steak rest for 5 minutes, then cut into pieces or slices. Season with a drizzle of extra virgin, sea salt (or a pinch of Profumo del Chianti), and pepper and serve on a wooden cutting board.

CHIANTI "TUNA" PORK

SERVES 4 TO 6

2½ pounds boneless pork shoulder, cut into 4-inch chunks

¼ cup coarse sea salt

2 cups dry white wine

1 sprig fresh rosemary

1 sprig fresh sage

6–8 fresh bay leaves

3 garlic cloves

1½ cups quality extra virgin olive oil

Sprinkle the pork chunks with 2 tablespoons of the salt, put them in a glass or ceramic container, and mix with 2 tablespoons of water. Cover with plastic wrap and refrigerate for at least 12 hours and up to 2 days.

Rinse the meat and put it in a casserole with the wine and enough water to cover the meat by 1 inch. Place over low heat and bring to a simmer. (This will take a long time.) Add the remaining 2 tablespoons salt, the rosemary, sage, 3 bay leaves, and 2 garlic cloves; simmer for 1½ to 2 hours or until tender. Let the pork cool completely in the broth.

Remove the pork from the broth, place in a strainer, and drain for 30 minutes. Remove any exposed fat from the pork. Place the pork in a glass or ceramic container with the remaining bay leaves and remaining garlic clove, and cover with extra virgin. Marinate in the refrigerator for 12 hours or up to 3 or 4 days.

*   *   *

Lorenzo and Ludovica Villoresi

LORENZO VILLORESI

Via De'Bardi, 14
50125 Firenze
Tel: +39-055-234-1187
Fax: +39-055-234-5893
info@lorenzovilloresi.it
www.lorenzovilloresi.it
Visits by appointment only.

LORENZO VILLORESI is a Florentine "nose," a creator of custom fragrances whose atelier is on the top floor of a medieval tower in Florence's Oltrarno neighborhood. Entering the building is an olfactory preview: an intoxicating scent livens up the dreary entrance, the elevator ride, and the short flight of stairs to the studio door. The front room is dominated by shelves containing countless brown glass bottles of essences, extracts, distillates, and synthetics ("Sometimes they're better," explained Lorenzo), all waiting to be blended by the master. Lorenzo makes custom perfumes as well as his own line of scents, sold as perfume, cologne, soap, shampoo, conditioner, body cream, or oil. Lorenzo's newest line, Olea Europaea, is made with olive oil and smells like olive leaves, oil, and trees—perfect for someone with my extra virgin obsession. Old-fashioned cupboards display bottles of room fragrance to diffuse on a terra-cotta ring (it sits on a lightbulb), scented candles in frosted glass or alabaster tumblers (intricate veins in the stone are illuminated by the candlelight), and various room fresheners and potpourris. Lorenzo's wife Ludovica assists with sales, though less often since the births of their three children.

Lorenzo designed two perfumes for me: a savory one based on herbs and savory flavors like fennel, rosemary, pepper, tomato leaves, and lemon; and a sweet one using ingredients like vanilla, caramel, and spice. One at a time, he held a paper wand daubed with an essence or extract and asked how I liked it, and how I thought it would go with the others, adding drops of liquid to a beaker on a gram-scale, writing down the amounts, swirling the contents, giving me more wands to smell. It took four sessions to get the perfumes right, and then they had to ripen for a few months, but it didn't take that long to become friends with Lorenzo and Ludovica, and their atelier is only a few blocks from my home.

Lorenzo's recipe is like a perfume for lamb, inspired by ancient Roman flavors, sweet, sour, and spicy. Lorenzo's notes were longer than the recipe—laurel leaves, *laurus noblis,* not bay; cumin from Africa or the Middle East, *cuminun cyminum,* not simpler *carum carvi;* Mediterranean, not ocean salt; bitter or delicate honey. He recommends serving the lamb with boiled emmer (*farro*) or rice.

LAMB WITH ANCIENT ROMAN–INSPIRED MARINADE

MAIN COURSE

SERVES 4

¼ cup honey (either bitter, like chestnut, or mild, like orange blossom)

⅔ cup full-bodied red wine

1–2 tablespoons freshly ground cumin seeds

2 teaspoons sea salt

1 or 2 pinches grated nutmeg

2–4 fresh laurel (*laurus noblis*) leaves

Freshly ground chili pepper to taste

2 garlic cloves, smashed with the back of a knife

¼ cup fresh orange juice

1½–2 pounds boneless lamb shoulder or shank, cubed

2 tablespoons extra virgin olive oil

Heat the honey until it melts, then combine with the red wine, cumin, salt, grated nutmeg, laurel leaves, chili pepper, garlic cloves, and orange juice. Set aside.

Put the lamb cubes in a glass (or nonreactive) bowl, and mix well with the marinade. Refrigerate for 2 to 4 hours.

Preheat the oven to 375°F.

(recipe continues)

Remove the meat from the marinade, reserving the marinade, and pat dry with paper towels. Heat the extra virgin in a heavy-bottomed ovenproof pot. Sauté the meat until it loses its raw look, then pour the marinade over the meat. Cover the pot and bake in the oven for 1 to 2 hours, stirring every 15 minutes. Add a few tablespoons of hot water if the pot looks too dry.

Lorenzo Guidi

NANAMUTA

Corso Italia, 35

50123 Firenze

Tel: +39-055-267-5612

Fax: +39-055-265-7881

www.nanamuta.it

Lunch Monday–Friday, dinner every evening; open late every evening for after-theater.

All credit cards accepted.

A PRESS DINNER that paired champagne with tripe and innards was the inauspicious occasion of my first acquaintance with Lorenzo Guidi. In spite of the evening's gastronomic drawbacks (offal in every course but dessert, no vegetables), I enjoyed his restaurant, Nanamuta, and promised to come back, since the menu looked promising. It's now one of my favorites in Florence—inexpensive at lunchtime and featuring a more expanded menu in the evening. The focus is on classics like Florentine steak, perfectly fried foods (especially *coccoli*, or tiny dough crisps), spaghetti with clams, and ribollita in the winter. The wine list offers lots of surprises. Lorenzo's weighted-down-with-a-brick treatment for chicken is a Tuscan classic, but he uses boned chicken breasts or thighs because "they cook faster than half a chicken with bones."

1 teaspoon fresh rosemary leaves

1 teaspoon fresh sage leaves

1 teaspoon fresh mint leaves

1 teaspoon fresh thyme leaves

1 tablespoon fresh basil leaves

1 strip lemon zest

1–2 chili peppers

1–2 garlic cloves

Fine sea salt

4 boned chicken breasts or 6–8 boned chicken thighs

1½–2 cups cherry tomatoes

3 tablespoons extra virgin olive oil

2 bricks

Mince the rosemary, sage, mint, thyme, 1 teaspoon of the basil, the lemon zest, as much chili pepper as desired, garlic, and 1 teaspoon sea salt together. Lorenzo says to chop with a knife, but cooks in a hurry may want to process everything. Sprinkle the herb mixture over the chicken, coating both sides. Put the chicken breasts and any leftover herbs in a plastic bag and let marinate in the refrigerator for 24 hours.

Cut the cherry tomatoes in half or quarters. Chop the remaining basil and add to the tomatoes. Season with sea salt and 1 tablespoon extra virgin and set aside.

Rinse the bricks and cover with aluminum foil. Or prepare two plates, each large enough to cover two chicken breasts, and two heavy weights (cast-iron pan, pot of water, bags of beans, boxes of rice, etc.—creativity helps). Lightly oil a ridged grill pan or a cast-iron pan large enough to hold the chicken. Place over high heat. When the pan is smoking, put the chicken in one layer and cover with the bricks (or the weighted plates).

(recipe continues)

Turn the heat down to medium and cook the chicken breasts for 2 to 4 minutes. Remove the bricks, turn the chicken over, replace the bricks, and finish cooking for another 2 to 4 minutes.

Let the chicken rest for 3 minutes, then cut diagonally into ½-inch slices. Drizzle with the remaining oil and serve with the tomatoes.

Massimo Tarli

M Y HUSBAND, Massimo, is a Florentine electronic engineer with Etruscan roots, who travels all over the world. He taught me about Tuscan food and wine, and he brainwashed me with extra virgin. When we first dated, he brought me special treats to try from home: a taste of just-pressed olive oil, a piece of pecorino cheese, walnuts from the Mugello area north of Florence—all foods I had tasted before but in highly inferior versions. I fell in love.

When Massimo was growing up, his parents, sister, grandparents, aunts, uncles, and cousins all lived in the same apartment building in Florence, and they often ate together. One of Massimo's chores was to mince the herb mixture for the *Aristá,* or Roast Pork Loin, using a mezzaluna, the two-handled crescent-shaped knife that's safe for kids to use, since both hands are behind the blade. His grandfather Carlo would push (the verb in Tuscan is *pillottare*) the herb mix into slits cut into the pork loin. It's a job that Massimo still enjoys whenever I make *Aristá.* I have a kitchen hearth with a wind-up spit-roaster, so I can simply thread the meat onto the spit to turn slowly in front of an open fire for hours, the skin turning golden brown and crispy, perfuming the kitchen. But even a skinless pork loin roasted in the oven is a delicious option. Use the best pork you can find—consider ordering a skin-on loin from Niman Ranch (www.nimanranch.com).

ROAST PORK LOIN

SERVES 8 TO 10

6 garlic cloves

3–4 tablespoons fresh rosemary leaves

2 teaspoons fine sea salt and freshly ground black pepper

4–5 pound pork loin, boned, meat reassembled on the bone and
    tied firmly, preferably by your butcher

Mince the garlic and rosemary together and combine with the sea salt
and pepper. Insert a paring knife blade fully into the end of the pork loin,
working from both ends, and stuff the slit with the garlic-herb mixture,
saving a tablespoon to rub on the outside of the loin. Let the meat rest
for 30 minutes or more. (It can be prepared in advance and refrigerated.
Let come to room temperature before cooking.)

Preheat the oven or roaster to 325°F.

Insert the spit at the center of the loin and fix well to the spit, or place
on a rack in a roasting pan. Roast for 1½ to 2 hours, to an internal temperature of 140 to 145°F. Remove from oven and let rest 10 to 15 minutes, then untie the roast.

Cut the meat in ¾-inch slices and cut each slice in half or thirds. Cut
the bones into ribs and serve if you like.

✳   ✳   ✳

Alfonsina Ricchi

ALFONSINA RICCHI, wife of Enzo (page 154), is known to everyone in the neighborhood as Fonzie. A jack-of-all-trades at the family bar/restaurant in Piazza Santo Spirito, she bakes desserts, makes gelato, lends a hand in the kitchen at lunchtime (in the evening a hot young chef prepares more expensive, elaborate food including fish and seafood), and chats with locals from her perch in the cash register booth. We exchange recipes, neighborhood gossip, products I've brought back from my travels. Like me, Fonzie's a big fan of the seasonal produce the Innocenti brothers (page 148) sell at their market stand, and she always threatens to get there before me to buy all the good stuff (impossible, since I'm generally there at 7:30 A.M.). One spring morning, while the brothers were bagging my vegetables and herbs, we stood there together, inhaling the fresh herbal perfumes. Fonzie confessed that she'd like to make love to her husband in a field of basil. I must admit the scent *is* intoxicating.

CAFFÈ RICCHI
Piazza Santo Spirito 8/R
50125 Firenze
Tel: +39-055-215-864
info@caffericchi.it
www.caffericchi.it
Open 7 A.M.–1 A.M.; closed on
Sundays except the second Sunday
of the month. Closed for vacation
February 2–15 and August 2–15.

Enzo appreciates Fonzie's home-style cooking, and she makes special dishes for him at the restaurant with the Innocentis' seasonal vegetables, never listed on the menu, but highly requested by fans who include my husband and me. In Italy, turnips are sold with their greens attached, and Fonzie cooks both until tender, then sautés them in first-rate extra virgin with garlic and chili pepper, a typical Italian treatment.

SIDE DISH

TURNIPS AND THEIR GREENS WITH GARLIC AND CHILI PEPPER

SERVES 4 TO 6

1–1½ pounds turnip greens or broccoli rabe
1–2 medium turnips (4–6 ounces)
3 tablespoons coarse sea salt, plus more as needed
2–3 garlic cloves
Minced fresh chili pepper or red pepper flakes to taste
3–4 tablespoons extra virgin olive oil

Swish the greens in a sinkful (or large pot) of warm water to remove all dirt and grit. Drain.

Remove any bruised leaves and strip away any tough stems. Peel the turnips and cut into ½-inch cubes.

Bring 4 quarts of water to a rolling boil, add the salt and the greens, and cook 3 to 5 minutes, or more until tender—press a stem to see if it's soft. Remove the greens from the pot, place in a colander set into a sinkful of cold water to rapidly cool the greens. Drain them, squeeze to remove most of the water, chop coarsely, and set aside.

Cook the diced turnips in boiling water for 5 minutes, or until tender. Remove turnips from the water, place in a colander, and run cold water over them to cool. Reserve 1 cup of the cooking water.

Mince the garlic and hot pepper together and put in a little pile in a large nonstick skillet. Drizzle 2 tablespoons of extra virgin over the garlic-chili mixture and place the skillet over medium heat. Cook until the garlic barely begins to color. Add the cooked greens and turnips, stir in ½ cup of the cooking water, and cook until the liquid has evaporated. Taste for salt, adding more if necessary. Drizzle with additional extra virgin before serving.

Benedetta Vitali

BENEDETTA VITALI, chef-owner of the wonderful restaurant Zibibbo, in Florence, began her cooking career with Fabio Picchi as the wife/partner/chef of Cibrèo (page 109). We met at the restaurant—I'd stop by to chat when I shopped at the Sant'Ambrogio market. We talked, naturally, about food and our love for southern Italy, and we became friends. I helped in the kitchen for dinners that she and Fabio cooked in New York, San Francisco, and at Palazzo Medici-Riccardi in Florence. She always made desserts, but now she's single, has a place of her own, and has expanded her horizons beyond the dessert course.

ZIBIBBO

Via Terzollina, 3/r
50129 Firenze
Tel: +39-055-433-383
zibibbofirenze@libero.it
www.zibibbonline.com
Open Monday–Friday, 8 A.M.–
11 P.M.; Saturday 8 P.M.–12 A.M.;
Sunday 10 A.M.–3 P.M. Closed
during August.

Zibibbo's menu has some of Benedetta's favorites, developed at Cibrèo, but also fresh ravioli and spaghetti, which Cibrèo never served. Her cooking is lusty, homestyle, with vegetables from nearby farmers cooked until they're tender, not crunchy, with fully developed flavors. The wine list is personal, with unknown gems from southern Italy and interesting organic (some biodynamic) wines.

Benedetta wrote a fantastic cookbook, *Soffritto,* published by Ten Speed Press, allowing readers to re-create the experience of dining at her restaurant. A few jars of Zibibbo's homemade products, like orange peel in Port or spicy pear mostarda chutney, are wonderful souvenirs of dining at the restaurant. Fans should plan to sign up for her cooking lessons—for the schedule and more information about the restaurant, visit www.zibibbonline.com.

Benedetta gave me her recipe for Broccoli and Cauliflower Sformatino, or "little unmolded," but it's neither unmolded nor little. It's a creamy, chunky broccoli and cauliflower gratin that can be prepared in advance and baked at the last minute. Benedetta serves this as an appetizer, a few spoonfuls on a plate, but I like to serve it as a side dish.

SIDE DISH

BROCCOLI AND CAULIFLOWER SFORMATINO

SERVES 6 TO 8

¾ pound head of cauliflower
¾ pound broccoli
Coarse sea salt
1 cup milk
3 tablespoons butter or extra virgin olive oil
¼ cup all-purpose flour
¾ cup grated Parmigiano-Reggiano cheese
Freshly ground black pepper

Break the cauliflower into florets. If they're large, cut each of them into bite-size pieces. Cut the tops off the broccoli, trim the stems of the tough outer parts, and cut into ½-inch pieces. If the tops are large, cut into bite-size pieces.

Bring 6 quarts of water to a rolling boil; add 3 tablespoons coarse sea salt and the cauliflower. Cook for 10 to 12 minutes or until tender, not al dente. Remove the cauliflower from the pot, place in a sinkful of cold water to cool, then drain the cauliflower.

Put the broccoli stem chunks in the boiling water and cook for 7 minutes, then add the broccoli tops and cook for another 7 minutes or until tender. Remove broccoli from the pot and place in a sinkful of water to cool, then drain and combine with the cauliflower in a large bowl. Set aside 1 cup of the vegetable-cooking water.

Preheat the oven to 375°F.

Heat the milk and vegetable-cooking water in a small pot. Melt the butter in a small pot, add the flour, and stir over low heat for a few minutes but don't let the mixture color. Add the hot milk and stir energetically with a whisk until smooth and creamy. Remove from the heat, stir in the Parmigiano-Reggiano, and season with salt and pepper.

Combine the sauce with the broccoli and cauliflower and transfer the mixture to a baking dish, smoothing to a 2-inch layer. Bake for 20 to 25 minutes, until bubbling. Cool for 5 minutes before serving.

Carlo and Delfina Cioni

DA DELFINA is an old-fashioned super-Tuscan restaurant set amid vineyards and olive trees in the Carmignano area west of Florence. Delfina Cioni's husband was the game warden at the Medici villa of Artimino. He'd take the owner and his friends on hunting excursions and bring both the game and hunters home to his wife, who would cook dinner, which she served at tables in her living room, assisted by her son Carlo. Twenty years ago they moved the restaurant to a nearby farmhouse, and now Carlo works with his nephew Riccardo Peruzzi. Delfina, at ninety-six, still helps out in the kitchen and can often be found in the front room next to the hearth, with guinea hens and skewers of meat slowly spinning in the spit-roaster. When I taught at Tenuta di Capezzana (page 000), I'd always take my students for lunch at Da Delfina, and Carlo would do a spit-roasting demo for us starring guinea hen, wild fennel, and pancetta. While the birds spit-roasted, we'd go shopping for pottery in nearby Montelupo, then return to Da Delfina for lunch, dining in one of four beamed or brick-vaulted rooms decorated with prints, hunting trophies, and farm implements.

Visit Da Delfina the next time you're in Florence for a perfect Tuscan meal. The menu changes often and features wild and cultivated vegetables and herbs. Begin with a flan (*sformato*) of broccoli rabe or nettles or classic crostini with poultry liver pâté. Homemade pasta, like tortelli stuffed with potato or wide strips of maccheroni sauced with braised duck, are tasty, but don't miss Da Delfina's unusual version of ribollita, or bread-thickened soup sautéed in extra virgin olive oil to form a light, crisp crust. Main-course offerings include rabbit braised with olives and pine nuts, spit-roasted guinea hen or beef, and classic Florentine steak. Look for seasonal vegetables like porcini mushrooms, wild salad greens, broccoli rabe with chickpeas, or Fried Green Tomatoes with Grapes.

RISTORANTE DA DELFINA

Via della Chiesa, 1
59015 Artimino (PO)
Tel: +39-055-871-8074 or
+39-055-871-8119
Fax: +39-055-871-8175
posta@dadelfina.it
www.dadelfina.it
Closed Sunday evenings and all day Monday and from January 20–February 10 and all of August.
No credit cards.

Desserts like custard gelato with fruit sauces and almond biscotti are served with local Vin Santo dessert wine. The wine list features local Carmignano as well as a well-chosen selection of non-Tuscan wines. In the meantime you can make their recipe for green tomatoes until you have a chance to visit.

FRIED GREEN TOMATOES WITH GRAPES

SERVES 4 TO 6

¾ pound grapes (Delfina uses wine grapes, but use the best dark
    grapes you can get)
8 firm green tomatoes
Soft wheat flour (Italian "00" or White Lily flour), for coating slices
½ cup extra virgin olive oil
8 garlic cloves, mashed
Salt and freshly ground black pepper
2 tablespoons tomato sauce

Squeeze the juice from half the grapes (I process them, then mash them in a strainer to get around 6 tablespoons juice). Cut the remaining grapes in half (not necessary for smaller wine grapes). Cut the tomatoes into ½-inch slices (cut a slim slice off the top and bottom of the tomato so that all slices will have two wet surfaces) and remove the seeds (easy with a tomato knife or a grapefruit spoon). Heavily flour the slices.

    Heat the extra virgin in a large nonreactive skillet, brown the garlic, and remove. Add the tomato slices and fry until lightly browned on both sides. Season with salt and pepper, add the grape juice and the tomato sauce, and cook for a minute or two, then add the grapes and serve.

* * *

Lisa, Ugo, Benedetta, Beatrice, Vittorio, and Filippo Contini-Bonacossi; Patrizio Cirri

TENUTA DI CAPEZZANA

Via Capezzana, 100
59015 Carmignano (PO)
Tel: +39-055-870-6005
Fax: +39-055-870-6673
agriturismo@capezzana.it
www.capezzana.it
Visits by appointment only.

WHEN I WAS INVITED to visit Tenuta di Capezzana, a winery west of Florence that put Carmignano, one of Tuscany's great wines, on the map, it would be the start of a wonderful friendship. I was asked to stay for lunch, and like everyone else who's ever had the luck to dine at Capezzana, I was thrilled by the food prepared by Countess Lisa Contini-Bonacossi. I was also charmed by her husband, Count Ugo, who jokingly complained that his wife's cooking was so good it distracted everyone from the wines. It was a lively place; the count and countess's children, Benedetta, Beatrice, Vittorio, and Filippo, are all involved with the estate's production of quality wine and extra virgin olive oil. Because frequently there were family members, friends, and visiting customers from all over the world at their tables, three dining rooms were always ready for unexpected guests and improvised meals, all paired with Capezzana's fine wines.

When the family decided to start a cooking school, they asked me to create and run it. I'd stay at Capezzana with participants for a week of cooking in the old-fashioned kitchen with a wood-burning oven and hearth, plus visits to nearby food artisans and to local extra virgin and wine tastings with Count Ugo and his daugher Benedetta, and a private tour of the Contini-Bonacossi collection, a separate part of the Uffizi. During the course of a session I'd often bump into the count and countess having breakfast at the kitchen table (didn't want to mess up the tables already set for lunch) in their robes. Countess Lisa told the guests ghost stories about the villa and added a twist of fantasy to many of the dishes she prepared, drawing on ingredients from the estate as well as last-minute inspiration. She has since retired from the kitchen. Chef Patrizio Cirri carries on her culinary tradition, and tourists can still visit the winery, taste and purchase Capezzana's wines and extra virgin, rent a room or a farmhouse on the estate, or arrange for a special meal. For those who can't visit Capezzana, Countess Lisa's *Torta della Nonna* will provide a taste of the estate. Her recipe incorporates ricotta and almonds, neither of which are found in the classic version. If your almonds are tasteless, a drop or two of almond extract will improve their flavor.

TORTA DELLA NONNA

DESSERT

SERVES 6 TO 8; MAKES A 9- TO 10-INCH TART

PASTRY

2 cups soft wheat flour (Italian "00" or White Lily flour)

⅔ cup butter cut into small pieces

⅓ cup granulated sugar

Pinch of sea salt

Grated zest of ½ lemon

1 jumbo egg yolk

FILLING

1 jumbo egg yolk

½ teaspoon vanilla extract

Scant ¼ cup granulated sugar

2 tablespoons soft wheat flour (Italian "00" or White Lily flour)

½ cup milk, heated but not boiling

¾ cup ricotta

½ cup almonds

2 tablespoons pine nuts

⅛ teaspoon almond extract (optional)

Confectioners' sugar, for dusting

(recipe continues)

Make the pastry. Place the flour, butter, sugar, salt, and lemon zest in a food processor. Pulse to combine. Pile the mixture on a clean work surface. Make a well in the center, add the egg yolk, and stir with your fingers or a fork to combine to make a smooth dough. Add a teaspoon of water if the dough is too dry.

Form the dough into two balls, flatten into disks, wrap each with plastic wrap, and refrigerate for 30 to 60 minutes.

Make the filling. In a bowl, whisk the egg yolk and vanilla with the sugar and the flour. Whisk 3 tablespoons of hot milk into the mixture until smooth and then stir it back into the milk in the saucepan. Bring slowly to a boil, then cook, whisking constantly, until thickened, 2 to 3 minutes.

Cool the cream quickly by placing the pan in a bowl of cold water or by spreading the cream on baking sheets. Cool completely.

Combine the pastry cream and ricotta in a food processor and process until smooth. Roughly chop the almonds and combine with the pine nuts. Fold the nuts into the pastry cream mixture. Add the almond extract if desired. Refrigerate until ready to use.

Preheat the oven to 375°F.

On a well-floured piece of parchment paper, roll a disk of the chilled dough into a 9- or 10-inch round and place on a flat pizza pan. Roll the second disk to the same size on a piece of floured plastic wrap.

Spread the nut custard on the bottom crust, leaving a 1-inch border. Turn the second round over the filling and peel away the plastic wrap. Press the edges of the dough to seal and form a decorative edge. Bake until golden, 40 to 45 minutes.

Cool on a rack, then dust with confectioners' sugar. Serve with a glass of Vin Santo.

＊　＊　＊

Lorenza Sebasti, Marco, Arturo, Norma, and Gemma Pallanti

I'VE ALWAYS loved the wines and extra virgin from Castello di Ama. I've attended press dinners and wine tastings at their villa in the heart of Chianti Classico territory. But when Lorenza Sebasti, daughter of one of the owners, took over the reins, she brought excitement, enthusiasm, and new ideas to the village of Ama. Lorenza is married to agronomist/enologist Marco Pallanti, and he's always crafted their Chianti Classico, crus Bellavista and Casuccia, as expressions of their territory; they're the kind of wines that make a dinner special. I'm crazy about the well-priced Rosato—it drinks like a well-structured Tuscan white and goes with everything. Marco is also responsible for the *frantoio* olive mill, where each November, superb extra virgin is pressed daily from just-picked olives. It's my very favorite olive oil: spicy, peppery, full-flavored, and expensive, but worth every penny. Dressed with Castello di Ama's extra virgin, any simply boiled, steamed, baked, or even raw vegetables are amazingly delicious. I can't live without it.

CASTELLO DI AMA
Fraz. Lecchi in Chianti
Localita' Ama
53013 Gaiole in Chianti (SI)
Tel: +39-0577-746-031
Fax: +39-0577-746-117
info@castellodiama.com
www.castellodiama.com
Visits by appointment only.

Lorenza and Marco have commissioned site-specific sculptures for the villa from cutting-edge modern artists like Pistoletto, Buren, Geers, and Kapoor—pieces that express the same sense of *terroir* as the Castello di Ama wines and extra virgin. Visitors can make an appointment to see the collection. (Ask for Donatella.)

Lorenza and Marco lived near the winery until their kids were born, when they moved to Florence, just around the corner from me. I feel like a surrogate aunt, and bring cool Band-aids back from the United States for Arturo, Norma, and Gemma, and they visit often on their way home from school. My sister Suzanne lives next door to the Sebasti-Pallanti family and she sees them even more than I do.

This grape tart is a favorite of Arturo's, made in the fall with dark red Sangiovese grapes. It is called *schiacciata,* which means "flattened down," and in Tuscany generally refers to flatbread—what everyone else calls focaccia. In the fall, during the grape harvest, Tuscans make a dessert or snack of bread dough, wine grapes, and sugar—an austere cake that's said to be of Etruscan origin. When baked at home, it's made with baking powder instead of yeast; however, the dough I've made contains honey, yeast, and Chianti (from Castello di Ama—we want our yeast to be happy, don't we?) and seems far more Etruscan in spirit. If you can't get wine grapes, use Concord or even black or red seedless grapes, which, if not strictly Etruscan, do have the advantage of being seedless.

DESSERT

ETRUSCAN GRAPE TART

SERVES 6 TO 8

1 package active dry yeast (2½ teaspoons)
¾ cup warm water
3 tablespoons Chianti—drink the rest with dinner
1 tablespoon honey
2½–2¾ cups soft wheat flour (Italian "00" or White Lily flour)
¼ cup Tuscan extra virgin olive oil, plus more for oiling the bowl
½ teaspoon fine sea salt
Around 1¾ pounds wine, Concord, or red Grace grapes
6 tablespoons sugar

Dissolve the yeast in the warm water, wine, and honey in a large bowl. Let sit for 10 minutes or until bubbles form. Stir in ¾ cup flour—it doesn't have to be smooth because lumps will dissolve. Cover and let rise for 1 hour.

Add the olive oil, salt, and 1½ cups flour, and knead dough until smooth and elastic. Add up to ½ cup additional flour if necessary so it isn't sticky. Shape into a ball, place in a lightly oiled bowl, cover, and let rise for 1½ hours.

Punch the dough down and divide into two pieces. Roll each piece out to a rough 10 by 16-inch rectangle. Place one rectangle on parchment paper on a cookie sheet (or use a nonstick cookie sheet), scatter the dough with half the grapes, and sprinkle with 3 tablespoons sugar.

Use the second rectangle of dough to cover the bottom layer. Sprinkle the remaining grapes on the dough, gently press the grapes into the dough, and sprinkle with 3 tablespoons sugar. Cover with plastic wrap and a dishtowel and let rise for 1 hour.

Preheat the oven to 400°F. Bake for 35 to 45 minutes or until dark brown. Remove from pan while still warm and spoon excess juice over the tart. Serve at room temperature.

Francesco and Elisabetta Pandolfini

EVEN BEFORE I visited Elisabetta and Francesco Pandolfini's bakery, Mattei, in Prato, I was well acquainted with their products because my husband Massimo's aunt Enza often brought me their cookies. Mattei has been in the Pandolfini family for three generations, and practice makes perfect. Just about every bakery in Tuscany sells cantucci, also called biscotti di Prato in the province of Florence, but Mattei's are the best, as are their Brutti-Buoni, a cookie more commonly called *brutti ma buoni* ("ugly but tasty"), although they're not really unattractive. Mattei's biscotti di Prato are rich with egg yolks, studded with whole almonds, and free of the artificial vanilla flavoring most other bakeries use. Their Brutti-Buoni are a solid mass of chopped almonds held together with egg whites, not the meringue-like cookies found elsewhere. The cookies come in a distinctive blue paper bag tied with a string: green for biscotti di Prato, red to denote Brutti-Buoni. Their *savoiardi* (ladyfingers) are per-

ANTONIO MATTEI

Via Ricasoli, 20/22
59100 Prato
Tel: +39-0574-257-56
Fax: +39-0574-366-50
antoniomattei@texnet.it
www.antoniomattei.it
Closed Monday, Sundays in July, and August 8–30.

fect for tiramisù, while the *filone candito* pastry, a candied-cherry and marzipan-topped loaf, appeals even to those who despise candied cherries.

At Mattei, a Rube Goldberg–like contraption pipes the Brutti-Buoni onto a sheet of edible paper, and tamps them with their distinctive dimple. I tried them at home and had great success, even without the special paper. It's a simple recipe and the perfect way to use leftover egg whites. Pair Brutti-Buoni with a glass of Vin Santo

DESSERT

BRUTTI-BUONI

MAKES 25 COOKIES

2 cups whole almonds, with skins
¼ cup pine nuts (if freshness is in doubt, toast them lightly but
    don't let them brown)
1¼ cups superfine sugar
3 egg whites, lightly beaten with a fork
2 tablespoons pastry flour

Preheat the oven to 350°F. Line a baking sheet with parchment paper or use a nonstick baking liner.

Combine the almonds, pine nuts, and sugar in a food processor and process until the mixture is the texture of coarse cornmeal. Pour into a bowl, mix with the egg whites to combine, add the flour, and mix until absorbed into dough.

Roll out into balls slightly larger than a walnut and place on the baking sheet, 1 inch apart. Press the tops to lightly flatten, indenting slightly, and pinch the sides so the cookies aren't quite round. Bake for 12 to 15 minutes or until barely colored. Cool on the baking sheet for a few minutes, then transfer while still warm to a rack to complete cooling. The inside of the cookie should be moist. Store in an airtight tin.

Max Tarli-Willinger

M Y SON MAX grew up in Italy with an American mother and a Tuscan father, blending both traditions and languages. I toured through Italy with him in an early-model umbrella-stroller: compact, collapsible, but not built for cobblestone streets. We had to have it repaired at the *saldatore* (the man who solders) with great difficulty, since my Italian soldering vocabulary was rudimentary. Max went to nursery school in Rome while I learned to cook Roman style at the restaurant Silvano Paris and my husband, Massimo, did his compulsory military service. When we all moved to Florence, Max went to a public elementary school called Galileo Galilei. I learned Italian grammar, history, and geography from Max's schoolbooks. He grew up with a front yard full of olive trees, but he wore jeans and cowboy boots.

Max Tarli-Willinger does not receive visitors.

In our home, food was taken seriously, especially by me. We had tastings of all kinds of foods, brought back from trips throughout Italy— sweets that didn't get scarfed up by Max and his friends weren't worthy of note. But he made fun of me when, inspired by the San Pellegrino & Acqua Panna Water Codex (a highly informative book all about mineral water), we had a mineral water tasting, examining each glass for freshness, effervescence, structure, lightness, balance, unpleasant smells, and more. "It's just water," he complained. But he did give high votes to Panna, Tuscan still spring water from an Apennine aquifer. Me too. How could we resist delicious Tuscan water?

Every year for his birthday, Max got to choose the dinner menu. It was always the same: pizza and brownies. Not exactly nutritionally sound, but a synthesis of Max's Italian and American heritage. Massimo, who believes that butter is a lipid for unevolved palates, convinced me to substitute already-liquid extra virgin for the melted butter in my brownie recipe. I had to fiddle with the recipe a bit, but Max and Massimo were pleased with the result, especially when I used the fine chocolate from Amedei (page 152). Tuscan brownies became a family tradition; when I have some of Gennaro Esposito's father's exceptional walnuts, they're a fantastic, but not critical, addition. Massimo feels that unsweetened whipped cream should be served on the side, to be spooned onto the brownies at the last minute.

Max is now grown up, living in Milan and selling television advertising. He visits often, and when he comes to celebrate his birthday, he still requests the same menu, which I'm more than happy to prepare. But I make his brownies all year long.

TUSCAN BROWNIES

MAKES 16 SQUARES

4 ounces finest quality (70 percent) bittersweet chocolate

⅓ cup extra virgin olive oil, plus more for preparing the pan

½ cup plus 1 tablespoon soft wheat flour (Italian "00" or White Lily
  flour), plus more for dusting the parchment

⅛ teaspoon sea salt

2 eggs, at room temperature

¾ cup superfine sugar

1 teaspoon vanilla extract

½ cup chopped walnuts (optional)

1 cup unsweetened whipped cream (optional)

Preheat the oven to 350°F. Line an 8-inch square baking pan with a lightly oiled and floured piece of parchment paper that's larger than the pan by 2 inches.

Melt the chocolate over hot water or in a microwave and whisk in the extra virgin. Cool the mixture.

Mix the flour with the salt. Beat the eggs and sugar until pale and thickened, around 5 minutes. Add the vanilla and chocolate mixture, and combine well. Fold in the flour and optional walnuts, then pour into the prepared pan.

Bake for 22 to 26 minutes. The top will be dry, though a toothpick inserted in the center will be wet. Cool completely, then cut into squares, using a knife with a serrated blade. Serve with whipped cream.

✳   ✳   ✳

Piermario and Paola Meletti Cavallari

PIERMARIO AND PAOLA Meletti Cavallari had an enoteca in Bergamo in the early '70s, after Piermario opted out of his programmed career as an accountant. They met a lot of cool winemakers, visited wineries, and decided that the lifestyle appealed. After checking out areas with enological potential, they bought a farm in the hills of Bolgheri, near the Tuscan coast, where they could sail and see the sun set into the sea. The farm, Grattamacco, was also close to the winery of Marchese Incisa della Rocchetta, who was creating a stir with his Sassicaia, a wine made with nontraditional cabernet, from a non-DOC zone of little importance, that was classified as table wine. The established vineyards at Grattamacco were planted with traditional red sangiovese and white trebbiano, but Piermario experimented with new varietals, selecting those suitable to his area and grafting them onto the old vines, as well as planting new vineyards that concentrated on different clones of reds sangiovese and cabernet and white vermentino. The Bolgheri area's potential became evident, and important wineries like Antinori, Frescobaldi, Mondavi, and Gaja purchased land and planted more vineyards. With the help of enological consultant Maurizio Castelli (page 101), Piermario's wines got even better.

Piermario and his wife, Paola, have undertaken a new adventure, making a traditional Tuscan red dessert wine called Aleatico on the island of Elba, at Tenuta delle Ripalte. There's also a resort there, Costa dei Gabbiani, with beaches, swimming pools, sports, and accommodations in the nineteenth-century villa or at one of the restored farmhouses, all surrounded by Tenuta delle Ripalte's vineyards.

Paola is a terrific cook, working with the organic bounty of her vegetable garden and orchard, and although there are some really fantastic restaurants nearby, everyone always wants to eat at Grattamacco. Paola

TENUTA DELLE RIPALTE

Localita' Ripalte
57031 Capoliveri (LI)
Tel: +39-0565-942-111
www.costadeigabbiani.it

GRATTAMACCO

Localita' Lungagnano
57022 Castagneto Carducci (LI)
Tel: +39-0564-990-448 or
+39-0564-990-496
Fax: +39-0564-990-498
info@grattamacco.it
www.grattamacco.it
Visits by appointment only.

brought me this delicious tart when she and Piermario once came for dinner. She dries figs, apricots, and plums from her trees, and lightly cooks them with apples, nuts, and Aleatico, which Piermario brought to accompany her dessert. If you can't find Tenuta delle Ripalte Aleatico, use Vin Santo by Capezzana, Isole e Oleana, or Castello di Ama.

APPLE AND DRIED FRUIT TART

SERVES 8 TO 10

PASTRY
2¼ cups soft wheat flour (Italian "00" or White Lily Flour)
Pinch of sea salt
¾ cup unsalted butter, cut into small pieces
¾ cup granulated sugar
Zest of ½ lemon
3 egg yolks

FILLING
4 medium tart apples
½ cup coarsely chopped pitted prunes
⅓ cup coarsely chopped dried apricots
¾ cup coarsely chopped dried figs
½ cup Aleatico or other Tuscan dessert wine
¼ cup coarsely chopped walnuts
2 tablespoons pine nuts
3 tablespoons coarsely chopped almonds
½ cup raw brown sugar
1–2 tablespoons unsalted butter, cut into tiny pieces

Make the pastry. Place the flour, salt, butter, sugar, and lemon zest in a food processor and pulse to combine. Pile the mixture on a clean work surface, make a well in the center, add the egg yolks, and stir with your fingers or a fork to make a smooth dough. Form the dough into two balls, one twice the size of the other. Wrap with plastic wrap and refrigerate for 30 to 60 minutes.

Preheat the oven to just below 400°F.

Make the filling. Peel, core, and cut the apples into small pieces. Combine the prunes, apricots, and figs with the Aleatico in a 3-quart pot and simmer over low heat for a few minutes to soften the fruit. Add the apples and cook for another 10 minutes or until the apples begin to soften. Add the walnuts, pine nuts, almonds, and brown sugar.

Place a piece of parchment paper in an 11-inch springform pan. (If you don't have an 11-inch pan, a 10-inch pan will do.) Roll out the larger ball of dough between two pieces of lightly floured plastic wrap into a 13-inch circle and place in the pan. Roll the smaller ball of dough into a circle thinner than the bottom crust. Place the filling in the pie shell, top with the butter, and cover with the second dough circle. Cut off excess dough and crimp the edges with fingers or a fork to seal and make an attractive border. Puncture the surface of the top crust with a fork in several places so that steam can escape. Bake for 40 minutes or until golden.

Valerio and Antonio Innocenti

PIAZZA SANTO SPIRITO

On Wednesday and Saturday mornings only—get there early. Come with me during one of my Market-to-Table sessions. www.faithwillinger.com

WHEN I MOVED to the city of Florence, I'd visit Torquato Innocenti (page 106) at his stand in the Santo Spirito market daily for great organic vegetables, Tuscan stories, and recipes. Torquato has since passed away, and though his sons Valerio and Antonio (who have other jobs) set up their stand only on Wednesdays and Saturdays, I'm relieved that they've chosen to maintain the family tradition, since I rely so heavily on their superb produce. I'm usually the first at their stand when it opens at 7:30; my husband refers to me as the vegetable warrior and asks how the war went when I come home to rejoin him in bed Saturday mornings. I take my Wednesday Market-to-Table cooking classes to visit the Innocenti brothers mid-morning, although I will have selected all the items to be used in my demos earlier that morning. Produce is weighed on an electronic scale that calculates in euros, a far cry from Torquato's day, but the bill is still written in pencil, added without the benefit of a calculator. And while Torquato related recipes, Valerio is more likely to talk about the environment, how the climate has changed, and the sudden abundance of "organic" produce.

In the spring, the Innocenti brothers' strawberries are picked ripe and sold in clear plastic baskets, stems and leaves fresh-looking; they are bright red and juicy all the way through when you take a bite, and smell like super-berries. It's not surprising that they sell out quickly. Antonio recommends marinating his strawberries with sugar, red wine, and maybe a little lemon zest. This classic Italian preparation is simple, but first-rate, seasonal strawberries are a must. Peaches, on the other hand, are sold sun-ripened and sweet, but either soft if they are to be used quickly or hard if to be used in a day or two. Torquato always recommended misting the peaches on a plate to facilitate the softening process.

STRAWBERRIES OR PEACHES WITH WINE

SERVES 3 TO 4

1 pint strawberries or 4 large peaches

2–4 tablespoons sugar

½ cup dry red wine (something good enough to drink)

1 strip lemon zest

Clean the berries or peel the peaches. Quarter the berries or slice them into a bowl or slice the peaches into a bowl. Sprinkle the fruit with sugar (add more if you really want to be Italian), add the red wine and lemon zest, and marinate for 10 minutes but no longer than 30 or the fruit will get soggy. Remove the lemon zest and serve.

Zia Enza Tarli

ENZA TARLI, my father-in-law's sister, is the Tuscan *zia* (aunt) of my dreams. She's an expert on family traditions, knows about obscure Italian holidays and festivities, and is a fantastic cook. Retired from her job in the textile business, she devotes a great deal of her time to her extended family—my husband, his sister, their companions and offspring. She doesn't trust electricity or anything invented after the iron; she gave away her washing machine since she prefers washing by hand on a scrub-board—even sheets and jeans. Although she doesn't own a TV, she stays well informed by listening to the radio and calls regularly to tell us about upcoming bus or train strikes. Whenever she comes for Sunday lunch Aunt Enza brings her sewing kit, just in case anything needs to be repaired, and she always takes the tablecloth and napkins home after lunch to wash and iron them.

Aunt Enza does not receive visitors.

It's not surprising that her cooking is simple. She chops everything by hand and has never turned on her oven (it's new; she's not sure she can trust it), but Enza's tried-and-true classics never fail to please. Her crostini with hand-chopped livers are unbeatable, and we're wild about her fritto misto—a medley of chicken, vegetables, and bread (dipped in the leftover batter from the chicken and vegetables), all deep-fried in the same good Tuscan extra virgin she uses to dress our salads. But everyone's favorite is Enza's Tiramisù, which she makes for all family get-togethers and presents with *"Auguri"* (Best Wishes) written in bits of chopped chocolate on top. Her easy recipe is the best, and always a big hit.

3 eggs, separated (see Note)

5 tablespoons sugar

1½ cups mascarpone

4 ounces soft ladyfingers

1 cup unsweetened brewed espresso (8–10 shots), cooled

Unsweetened cocoa or bittersweet chocolate, for garnish

Beat the egg whites with 1 tablespoon of the sugar until soft peaks form. In another bowl, beat the egg yolks with the remaining 4 tablespoons sugar until thick and pale yellow. Add the mascarpone to the egg yolk mixture and blend until well combined. Lightly fold the egg whites into the mascarpone mixture.

Dip the ladyfingers, one at a time, in the espresso and line the bottom of a 2-quart bowl or serving dish with about one-third of the cookies. Cover with about one-third of the mascarpone mixture. Continue building the tiramisù, making three layers of cookies topped with three layers of mascarpone mixture. Dust the finished tiramisù with unsweetened cocoa or chop up some bittersweet chocolate and use it to spell out a message on top, as Enza does. Refrigerate at least 2 hours.

NOTE: This recipe contains raw eggs and is not appropriate for pregnant women, immuno-compromised patients, the very young, or the elderly.

* * *

Alessio and Cecilia Tessieri

AMEDEI

Via San Gervasio, 29

56020 La Rotta (Pontedera) (PI)

Tel: +39-0587-484-849

Fax: +39-0587-483-208

amedei@amedei.it

www.amedei.it

Visits by appointment only.

BROTHER AND SISTER Alessio and Cecilia Tessieri make my favorite chocolate in the world, Amedei. Alessio goes straight to the source, buying cocoa beans in their countries of origin throughout South America and the Caribbean; Cecilia is the blender, and she creates the flavor combinations for their pralines. Amedei makes white, milk, and bittersweet chocolates, but their specialties are single-country cru chocolate from Venezuela, Ecuador, Jamaica, Grenada, and Trinidad in different percentages of bittersweet—63, 66, and 70 percent; and single-bean Porcelana and Chuao, the most prized chocolate beans in the world. At the Amedei factory in the countryside not far from Pisa where the beans are processed, the Tuscan rusty-pink façade is painted with cocoa bean leaves and pods.

Most of the world's rare, rich-tasting Chuao cocoa beans come from an inaccessible region on a Venezuelan peninsula. A French middleman had the exclusive rights to these beans, which he bought and resold to important chocolate makers, who used them in their blends. Alessio wanted to use the beans as a single-cultivar chocolate; he tried to get them through official channels, but as an Italian chocolate maker, he wasn't taken seriously. Instead, he went to the Venezuelan farmers' cooperative and offered a higher price as well as the collaboration of an agronomist to improve the quantity and quality of the beans. He also promised to provide bright red uniforms for the cooperative's baseball team, which was probably the clincher. Amedei now buys all the Chuao beans grown by the cooperative.

Alessio and Cecilia are fanatical about cocoa and about cocoa beans. Once I visited their factory, saw the process, and tasted their chocolates, I was hooked as well. Even my husband, who never eats sweets, can't live without the individually wrapped squares of Amedei. I bake with Chuao or Tuscan Black 70 percent bittersweet chocolate, and use it to make hot chocolate, gelato, and a superlative dark chocolate sauce. It would be an insult to the greatest bittersweet chocolate to add cream and butter, diluting the flavor and essentially making it into milk chocolate. Alessio's recipe for chocolate sauce enriched with extra virgin treats the intense, long-lasting flavors of Amedei's fine chocolate with Tuscan respect. Those who like mocha flavoring may substitute espresso for ¼ cup of the water and increase the sugar to ⅓ cup. This sauce is especially good with an ice cream or gelato.

REALLY BITTERSWEET TUSCAN CHOCOLATE SAUCE

DESSERT

MAKES APPROXIMATELY 1½ CUPS SAUCE

6 ounces best-quality (70 percent) bittersweet chocolate,
    preferably Amedei
¼ cup sugar
½ teaspoon vanilla extract
Pinch of sea salt
2 tablespoons extra virgin olive oil

Combine the chocolate, 6 tablespoons water, sugar, vanilla, and salt in the top of a double boiler and melt over hot water. (Or melt in a microwave.) Whisk the ingredients together. (Sauce can be prepared in advance.) Before serving, whisk the extra virgin, a tablespoon at a time, into the warm chocolate mixture. Serve warm.

* * *

Enzo and Alfredo Ricchi; Alessandra Tancredi

CAFFÈ RICCHI

Piazza Santo Spirito, 8/R
50125 Firenze
Tel: +39-055-215-864
info@caffericchi.it
www.caffericchi.it
Open 7 A.M.–1 A.M. Monday–
Saturday; closed Sundays except
second Sunday of the month.
Closed February 2–15
and August 2–15.

C AFFÈ RICCHI, in Piazza Santo Spirito in Florence, is my neighborhood hangout. Locals stop in for a breakfast of cappuccino and pastry or for an espresso or snack any time of day; at lunchtime the tables are set with paper placemats and hot dishes are served. In the spring, summer, and fall there's seating outside under an awning, with a great view of the church. The bar's walls, as well as a side room, are decorated with drawings of the façade of Brunelleschi's Santo Spirito church, rendered according to the imaginations of the architects, artists, and locals who entered a fanciful competition to "finish" the unadorned façade.

Enzo Ricchi and his uncle Alfredo preside over the cash register station, across from the bar. Enzo's wife, Alfonsina (page 127) works all stations, and makes desserts, gelato, and cocktail snacks. Alessandra Tancredi, who works behind the bar in the evening, specializes in cocktails, and cocktail hour at Ricchi is a great time of day. The counter is lined with crostini, sun-dried tomatoes and cheese on toothpicks, hot dips with crackers, and prosciutto or salami wrapped around fruit, cheese, or bread. Alessandra makes classic and inventive cocktails, the most popular of which are the Negroni and variations on that theme.

The Negroni was invented by Count Camillo Negroni in Florence around 1920. The rage at the time was for a cocktail called the Americano, made of equal parts red vermouth and Campari, splashed with soda water. The count asked barman Fosco Scarselli to fortify his Americano with gin and add half an orange slice as a garnish, and the drink caught on. Enzo's take on the Americano replaces the classic Martini Rosso vermouth with Carpano—I call it the Tosco-Americano. Another cool variation, the Sbagliato (past particple of the Italian for "to mistake"), is simply an Americano made with sparkling wine instead of soda.

Although Enzo doesn't cook—Alfonsina is the talent in the kitchen—he's capable of preparing a classic Tuscan appetizer of salami and figs that requires almost no effort. Those without access to fresh figs can use quality dried figs, split in half.

CAMPARI COCKTAILS WITH SALAMI AND FIGS

SERVES 1

3–4 ice cubes
1 ounce Campari
1 ounce Martini Rosso vermouth (or Carpano, for Enzo's Tosco-
   Americano)
Splash of seltzer or soda water (or sparkling wine for Sbagliato)
1 ounce gin, for those who want a Negroni
½ orange slice

Put the ice cubes in an old-fashioned cocktail glass. Add the Campari, Martini Rosso or Carpano vermouth, and seltzer or soda water (or sparkling wine for the Sbagliato) and gin (for those who want a Negroni), and stir. Garnish with ½ orange slice.

2 fresh or quality dried figs
Fennel seeds, lightly crushed
4 thin slices good-quality Italian-style salami

Halve the figs and sprinkle with a few fennel seeds. Wrap each half with a slice of salami and secure with a toothpick.

* * *

Lucia Andreotti and Giorgio Maffucci

LUCIA ANDREOTTI AND GIORGIO MAFFUCCI

Found in Piazza Santa Spirito on the second and third Sunday of every month except August or at their agriturismo.

L'ALBERACCIO

Località Lolle, 5
51020 Lolle, Piteglio (PT)
Tel/Fax: +39-0573-691-35

THE SECOND Sunday of each month a market is held in Piazza Santo Spirito, not far from my home in Florence, that draws large crowds of shoppers. The market is fun, with stands selling costume jewelry, cutlery, wooden tools, flowers and plants, and half-price books. There's a truck selling candy, nuts, and *brigidini* (anise wafer cookies), another with a whole roast pig, and hot dogs and hamburgers sizzling on a grill. Lucia and Giorgio have a simple wooden stand there, where they make the delicious, traditional Tuscan snack known as *necci*, or chestnut-flour pancakes served plain or spread with ricotta. Giorgio pours batter onto a long-handled flat iron disk that's been heating over a burner, tops it with another hot disk, and flips the whole thing over on the burner. Lucia spreads the finished *necci* with ricotta and chats with customers. One bite and we were friends.

Lucia and Giorgio have an *agriturismo* (a working farm that takes in lodgers) north of Pistoia, an area known for its fine chestnuts. Their chestnut harvest is ground into flour at a nearby mill. At the *agriturismo*, Lucia and Giorgio make *necci* the traditional way, over real coals in special terra-cotta dishes lined with chestnut leaves. My Tuscan friends love *necci* as is, but non-Tuscans may appreciate the addition of sugar (and maybe even raisins or chopped chocolate) to the ricotta. I'm sure that Lucia and Giorgio would be horrified, but I won't tell.

SERVES 4 TO 6

1½ cups ricotta (freshest possible, sheep's milk to be authentic)

2–3 tablespoons sugar (optional)

3 tablespoons raisins (soaked in water for 20 minutes to soften)
    or chopped bittersweet chocolate (optional)

1½ cups chestnut flour

Pinch of fine sea salt

1½ cups plus 1 tablespoon filtered water

Extra virgin olive oil (or a piece of salt pork
    if you want to be authentic)

Drain the ricotta if there's excess water. Purée in a processor or mash through a food mill or sieve. Transfer to a bowl and mix with a spatula until smooth enough to spread. Those with a sweet tooth can add optional sugar. If you are using the optional raisins or chopped chocolate pieces, stir them into the ricotta.

Whisk the chestnut flour, salt, and filtered water to make a smooth batter, thinner than pancake batter.

Pour a few drops of extra virgin on a paper towel or cloth (or use a chunk of salt pork without the towel) and rub in a 6-inch nonstick pan. Place the pan over medium-high heat and when hot, pour in ¼ cup of the chestnut batter and swirl around the pan to form a thin pancake. Cook until bubbles have formed and the pancake is dry around the edges. Turn it over (with the help of a plastic spatula) and cook the second side until the pancake stops steaming. Remove from pan, place on a paper towel cloth, and keep warm. Re-oil the pan before proceeding with the next pancake.

When all the pancakes are cooked, spread each with 2 tablespoons ricotta and roll into a tube. Serve immediately.

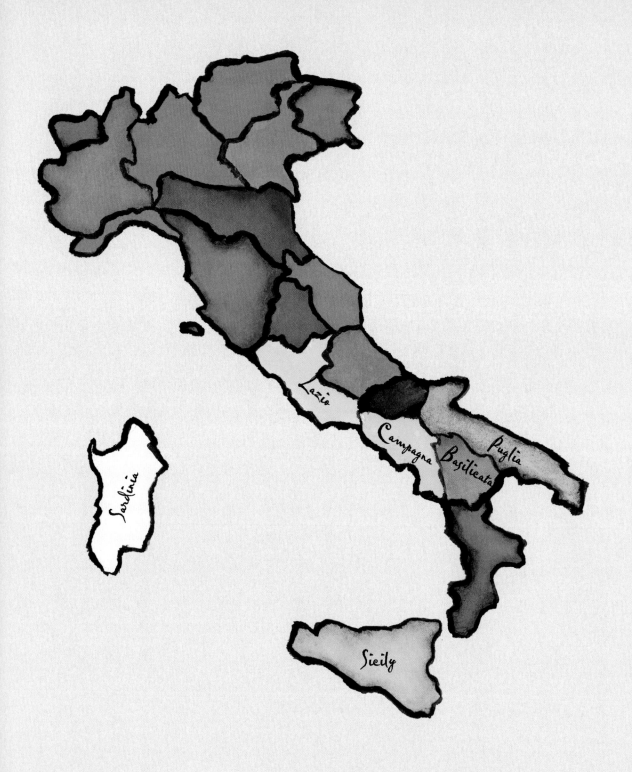

Lazio

Campagna

Basilicata

Puglia

Sardinia

Sicily

Southern Italy and the Islands

'VE BEEN LONGING to write about southern Italy and the islands, the regions not mentioned in *Eating in Italy,* because I've found some of the most exciting foods and wines I've ever tasted, and met the most incredibly generous people. Rome, where I lived for five years, was my gateway to these areas. I apprenticed in a Roman restaurant, and learned to love al dente pasta and non–al dente vegetables. My adventures in southern Italy often took me to a "time warp" experience, miraculous restaurants or food producers unaware of the twenty-first century. Naples and the region of Campania make my heart beat faster—is it the magnetic energy of Vesuvius or my love of pizza? A voyage to Sicily always makes me happy, and Calabria is right across the Strait of Messina. Puglia and Basilicata aren't easy to get to, but are well worth the schlep. Sardinia takes time to explore, and avoid the fancy beach resorts if you're interested in food. Friends and their recipes from Abruzzo and Molise didn't make the cut—I'll have to save that for my next book—but here is a selection of a few of my favorites from the irresistible south.

Leni and Mario Attanasio, Alois Lageder

LIKE THEIR FRIENDS Carla and Antonio Sersale, Leni and Mario Attanasio are hoteliers in Positano, where they own Palazzo Murat, a charming hotel with wonderful gardens. They know everyone in town, especially since Mario is a dentist. Leni is from Alto Adige—think Alps and Italian with a German accent—and her brother is winemaker Alois Lageder. She's fallen in love with Positano and has adapted to its leisurely Mediterranean pace and cuisine. Leni and Mario live in an apartment that's part of the palace with the original kitchen. There is a huge charcoal-burning cookstove, Mario's pet parrot in a cage in the corner, and signs of Leni's interest in cooking everywhere: ingredients, tools, baskets she's picked up on her travels. We had a snack of Alois's wine, bread, anchovies, and butter at the marble table in her kitchen, and as we talked about our favorite restaurants, the wine evaporated and we became friends. Since then she and Mario have come to my kitchen in Florence for dinner, and joined me on various culinary excursions.

When I told Leni which recipe I had chosen to represent her, she complained "too easy"; it was something she had served me when she was going out for dinner and hadn't prepared anything special. But each of her ingredients was local, chosen with care: great anchovies boned and marinated in extra virgin, quality butter made by local mozzarella producers who have found a use for the whey, and bread from a wood-burning oven. We drank Alois's Pinot Nero, and even though it wasn't local, it went well with the anchovies.

HOTEL PALAZZO MURAT

Via dei Mulini, 23

84017 Positano (SA)

Tel: +39-089-875-177

Fax: +39-089-811-419

info@palazzomurat.it

www.palazzomurat.it

Hotel is open from March 20 to the end of October; the restaurant is open from April 8 to November 2 for dinner only.

ALOIS LAGEDER

Vicolo dei Conti, 9

39040 Magrè (BZ)

Tel: +39-0471-809-500

Fax: +39-0471-809-550

info@lageder.com

www.lageder.com

Visits by appointment only.

ANCHOVIES AND BUTTER

SERVES 6

4 ounces anchovies, packed in salt, or quality anchovy fillets
    packed in oil (see Note)
½–¾ cup best-quality extra virgin olive oil
Rustic country-style bread, sliced
Unsalted butter, at room temperature

For packed-in-salt anchovies, brush off excess salt. Scrape off anchovy skin with a knife. Rip off the heads, remove the fins, and discard. Remove the top fillet of each by running your thumb, starting at the head end, along the spine, peeling off the fillet to the tail. Remove the central spine and attached bones in one piece. Run your fingers along the fillet to make sure all bones have been removed. Place in a nonreactive bowl and cover with extra virgin. Marinate for 2 to 3 hours, though they'll last a month if stored in a cool, dark place. (Those who can find quality anchovy fillets packed in oil from Italy or Spain should simply drain them and marinate in extra virgin olive oil.)

Serve the anchovy fillets at room temperature, with bread and unsalted butter.

NOTE: You can use the marinating oil for salads and in any dish in which you use anchovies.

Silvia and Anna Imparato

SILVIA IMPARATO owns Montevetrano, one of the most exciting wineries in southern Italy. As a photographer in Rome, Silvia had always loved wine; together with some wine-loving friends, she came up with the idea of making wine on her family's estate in Campania, not far from Salerno—not exactly an area known for fine wines. She hired a hot-shot enologist and planted native varietal aglianico along with cabernet and merlot. The wine was an instant success, called the Sassicaia of the south by wine expert Robert Parker, and became a cult favorite. A group of food-loving friends and I visited the *agriturismo* inn she runs with her sister Anna. It's called La Vecchia Quercia, and guests stay in stylishly rustic rooms or suites with kitchens. Everyone was enchanted with our accommodations and thrilled by breakfast—just-baked bread, local butter, mozzarella, and Montevetrano's special preserves in flavors like orange and prune, celery, eggplant, pumpkin, or bell pepper. Guests at La Vecchia Quercia can hang out at the pool, book a wine-tasting or cooking class, help out during the grape harvest, shop for the estate's fine

AZIENDA AGRICOLA MONTEVETRANO DI SILVIA IMPARATO

Via Montevetrano, 3
Localita' Nido, San Cipriano
Picentino 84099 (SA)
Tel: +39-089-882-285
Fax: +39-089-882-010
montevetrano@tin.it
www.montevetrano.it
Visits by appointment only.

LA VECCHIA QUERCIA

Via Montevetrano, 4
Campigliano, San Cipriano
Picentino 84099 (SA)
Tel: +39-089-882-528
Fax: +39-089-882-010
Cell: +39-335-784-3018
info@lavecchiaquercia.it
www.lavecchiaquercia.it

products (preserves, wine, hazelnuts, olives, citrus fruits), or even request (two days in advance) a special dinner accompanied by Montevetrano's spectacular wines.

I see Silvia at all the predictable wine events, drink her wine when I'm feeling flush (it's expensive), use the wonderful preserves, and dream about a return visit to La Vecchia Quercia. Silvia's recipe for pastries with pecorino and pepper preserve makes a lovely antipasto or garnish for fish, pork, or cheese dishes, and is quite a bit easier than the trip to San Cipriano Picentino.

ANTIPASTO

SAVORY PECORINO AND PEPPER PRESERVE PASTRIES

SERVES 4 TO 8

3 sheets frozen puff pastry, thawed
16 thin 2-inch-square slices of fresh pecorino cheese
8 teaspoons good-quality pepper preserves

Preheat the oven to 400°F.

Cut each piece of puff pastry in half lengthwise, then cut each strip into four squares. Trim the pecorino into squares slightly smaller than the puff pastry. Put a slice of pecorino on a square of pastry and top with ½ teaspoon of pepper preserves. Cover with another square of the puff pastry, top with pecorino and preserves, then top with a final layer of puff pastry. Repeat with the remaining pastry to make eight stacks.

Place the pastry stacks on a baking sheet lined with parchment paper or a nonstick mat. Bake for 10 to 12 minutes; pastry will be puffed and almost cooked. Remove from the oven, spread ¼ teaspoon pepper preserves on the top of each pastry, and return to the oven for 3 minutes, or until glazed and lightly browned. Serve immediately.

Antonello Colonna and Alessandro Pipero

Y FRIEND Paola di Mauro (page 189) told me I'd love Antonello Colonna and his restaurant in Labico, outside Rome, and as usual she was right. My first meal there began with a dish that's typical of Antonello: cabbage *sformato*. The word means "unmolded," but usually refers to a smooth vegetable purée, often bound with béchamel sauce. Here, sautéed cabbage was zapped with chili pepper and garlic, molded with spoons like quenelles, then topped with melty lardo fatback. The flavors were rustic, regional, and seasonal, and the presentation was simple. My meal was fantastic and I enjoyed Antonello's lively cooking as much as his jokes about fancy puréed (and usually tasteless) cuisine. The sommelier, Alessandro Pipero, approached his wine list with the same sense of gusto, and the Lazio section was filled with undiscovered gems.

ANTONELLO COLONNA

Via Roma, 89
00030 Labico (RM)
Tel: +39-06-951-0032
Fax: +39-06-951-1000
antonellolabico@antonello colonna.it
www.antonellocolonna.it
Closed Sunday nights and all day Monday; closed July 31–August 31.

Antonello invited me into the kitchen after lunch to meet his mother, where they showed me how to make spaghetti alla carbonara, and we became friends. So when I learned that Antonello was to be the judge at Scuochi, a competition in which journalists cook for a famous chef, I decided to take the challenge. I was the only non-Italian participant; the other journalists included a restaurant critic from a Milan newspaper, a writer from a financial monthly, and a correspondent from *Gambero Rosso,* the TV food channel and magazine. I brought Chianti "butter" (puréed fatback with garlic and herbs) from Dario Cecchini (page 116), wild greens from the Innocenti brothers' stand (page 148) at my local market, and super-Tuscan extra virgin, and made a series of crostini—toasted bread with toppings. The restaurant critic made a pseudo-Mongolian hot pot—not a big hit with the Italians. I sat next to Antonello, and he told me about his plans for the future, a move from the center of Labico to the outskirts of town, where he would create a most unusual gastronomical relais-spa. I can't wait. Antonello didn't give the dishes a final vote, but he wrote a poem about our efforts, seemingly praising everyone while subtly criticizing the Mongolian hot pot. To check out the dishes that we prepared, visit www.cinquesensi.it/scuochi/2004/Febbraio/QB_autori.asp.

Better yet, head for Antonello's restaurant. The relais, when it's built, should be the perfect gastronomic welcome to Italy, a great place to recover from jet lag after arriving in Rome.

CABBAGE SFORMATO

SERVES 4 TO 6

1 pound green cabbage

1 garlic glove

Red pepper flakes to taste

¼ cup extra virgin olive oil, plus extra for garnish

1–2 teaspoons coarse sea salt

4–6 tablespoons grated pecorino cheese

4–6 very thin slices cured lard or fatback

Fresh marjoram

Clean and core the cabbage, and slice into thinnest strips; this is easiest done with a mandoline. Put the garlic clove and red pepper flakes in a heavy-bottomed pot, drizzle with extra virgin, and place over medium heat. When the garlic begins to sizzle, add the cabbage and 1 teaspoon salt, and stir to coat the cabbage with the oil. Cook over low heat for up to 1 hour, until the cabbage is tender, adding a few tablespoons at a time of boiling water (up to ½ cup) if the cabbage starts to brown. Taste for salt and add more if necessary.

Using two large tablespoons, shape four to six ovals of the cabbage mixture. Top each with a tablespoon of grated cheese, drape with a slice of lard, then garnish with fresh marjoram and a drizzle of extra virgin.

* * *

Dora and Angelo Ricci

AL FORNELLO DA RICCI

Contrada Montevicoli, 71
72013 Ceglie Messapica (BR)
Tel/Fax: +39-0831-377-104
www.jre.it/italiano/b/
ristoratore.xtmlid=10.html
www.mangiarebene.net/CHEFS/
ricci/
Closed all of February and
September, plus Monday evening
and all day Tuesday.
All credit cards accepted.

M Y FIRST VISIT to Al Fornello da Ricci was love at first sight, although it wasn't easy to find, outside the city of Ceglie Messapica in the locality of Montevicoli. A *trullo,* one of the ancient circular stone dwellings in the area, next to the parking lot was a good sign for lovers of tradition, like me. Dora Ricci's cooking, pure Puglia, comes straight from the heart, and she uses the best local ingredients that her husband, Angelo, can find. A visit with Angelo and Dora is always a thrill; he's taken me to eat sea urchins on the beach near Torre Canne (in the province of Brindisi), to purchase ricotta and pecorino from a local shepherd, to a butcher who makes the best *salumi,* introduced me to winemakers and winery owners, and turned me on to some interesting restaurants. But best of all is Dora's cucina. She makes hard-wheat pasta like orecchiette, frusciddati, and cavatelli by hand, but she's modest about her skills, saying that the traditional dishes she prepares are simple so her seasonal and regional ingredients can shine. The dining rooms are rustic, attractive—comfortable tables set with local pottery and important wine glasses, a hint that Angelo Ricci really cares about wine.

A meal always begins with a plateful of tiny, addictive *polpettine,* eggplant stuffed with pecorino cheese, or regional *salumi.* First-course offerings include soups like grain and chickpea soup, classic fava purée and chicory, or Dora's hand-formed pasta dressed with vegetables. Main-course lamb and kid, in season, are roasted in the oven from which the restaurant gets its name. Cheese lovers will enjoy the local cheese selection that includes *ricotta forte,* a sheep's milk ricotta that's been fermented for a month—a strictly regional product that rarely makes it out of the region. Angelo's wine list is a pleasure to drink from, with Pugliese gems from Taurino and Rivera, as well as a fine selection of wines from the rest of Italy. Save room for delightfully uncomplicated desserts like almond tart, cookies, gelato, or sorbetti. Dinners usually conclude with one of Dora's homemade liqueurs flavored with herbs, rose petals, citrus, or coffee.

Dora and I speak often. She calls me Fede, a stand-in for Faith that's easier for most Italians (the "th" sound doesn't exist in Italian). We talk about her children who, with her blessings, are taking over the kitchen, with new techniques and ideas. "When are you coming to visit?" she always asks, but Ceglie isn't around the corner so I don't get there as much as I'd like to. But Dora visits my kitchen in spirit every time I make her little meatballs, and they disappear just as quickly at home as they do in the restaurant.

LITTLE MEATBALLS

ANTIPASTO

SERVES 6 TO 8

6 ounces ground beef, at room temperature
1 heaping cup freshly grated bread crumbs, made from stale
    but not dry rustic bread (I grate bread with the fine disk of the
    food mill)
¼ cup grated pecorino romano cheese
¼ cup chopped fresh parsley
2 eggs, at room temperature
1 garlic clove, minced
Sea salt and freshly ground black pepper to taste
1½–1¾ cups extra virgin olive oil, for frying

Place all the ingredients except the extra virgin in a bowl and mix gently until just combined. Don't overmix or meatballs will be tough. Form balls the size of marbles (around 1 teaspoon each).

Heat the oil in a 6-inch saucepan until very hot and fry the meatballs 6 to 8 at a time, in batches, until browned. Don't crowd the pan too much.

Drain the meatballs on paper towels and keep warm. Sprinkle with additional sea salt and serve hot.

Rita Denza

LA GALLURA

Corso Umberto, 145

07026 Olbia (SS)

Tel: +39-0789-246-48

Fax: +39-0789-246-29

Closed Mondays; closed December

20–January 6. All credit cards

except American Express.

RITA DENZA owns my favorite restaurant-hotel on Sardinia's northeast coast, in the city of Olbia. Local fishermen visit La Gallura daily, dropping off super-fresh, seasonal fish and spectacular seafood, and Rita knows how to do them justice. On a visit to La Gallura I spotted a plastic laundry basket of black spiky urchins, a jar of rose-colored urchin roe, three kinds of clams, wild oysters, mussels, bright red shrimp, and seafood I'd never seen before. The shelled limone di mare (*Microcosmus sulcatus*) looked like an oyster from another planet, its leathery gray flesh mottled with rusty mold. Rita split it into quarters to reveal a white cartilaginous interior with a center of rubbery, scrambled egg-like stuff she pried out with a fork. It was not on my new favorites list, unlike the delicious *orchiadas,* or sea anemones, the size of a euro coin that she dipped in a seawater and flour batter, then deep-fried. They tasted like delicate, tender clam bellies.

La Gallura has no menu, but I'd trust the staff to choose an appropriate meal. Check out the array of appetizer salads in the center of the main dining room. They're tempting enough to make a meal, but save room for the raw urchins, mussel salad, red mullet with wild fennel, spaghetti sauced with urchin roe or wild clams, and homemade pasta sauced with seafood and saffron or squid ink. Shrimp or whole fish are roasted in Rita's wood-burning stove, needing little but a drizzle of extra virgin to achieve pure perfection. I never resist Rita's gelato di riso, like an ice-cream version of rice pudding without the raisins. The wine list is quirky, with a fantastic selection of Sardinian wines as well as wines from "the continent," as Sardinians call the rest of Italy. La Gallura is always my first and last stop in Sardinia, for welcome and farewell meals—one is simply not enough. Rita gave me her recipe for an unusual mussel salad, a signature dish that's always among the offerings.

SERVES 4 TO 6

4 pounds mussels, cleaned

¼ cup mayonnaise, preferably homemade, with extra virgin
 olive oil

2 tablespoons Dijon mustard

3–4 drops Tabasco sauce

½ teaspoon mustard seeds

1 tablespoon white wine vinegar

1 tablespoon balsamic vinegar

1 cup yogurt, preferably goat's milk

2 teaspoons raw (Demerara) sugar

Sea salt

½ leek, trimmed and cut into julienne

1 celery rib, cut into julienne

Wash the mussels carefully and put in a large pot. Cook, covered, over high heat to open the shells—mussels will produce their own broth. Let the mussels cool. Save ½ cup of the mussel broth and strain it. Remove the mussels from their shells.

Combine the mayonnaise, mustard, Tabasco sauce, mustard seeds, vinegars, yogurt, and sugar. Season with salt. If the mixture is very thick (this will depend on the yogurt), reduce the mussel liquid and add a few spoonfuls to the sauce, which will be thick enough to coat the mussels.

Add the mussels, leek, and celery to the sauce and refrigerate for at least 1 hour.

* * *

Alfonso, Livia, Mario, and Ernesto Iaccarino

DON ALFONSO 1890

Corso Sant'Agata, 11

80064 Sant'Agata sui Due Golfi (NA)

Tel.: +39-081-878-0026

Fax: +39-081-533-0226

info@donalfonso1890.com

www.donalfonso.com

Closed Mondays. June 1–September 30: Tuesdays lunch only.

Usually closes for 2 months in the winter, usually January–March.

I MET LIVIA and Alfonso Iaccarino in the 1970s, when they were struggling restaurateurs and I was staying in Positano at Le Sirenuse. They had traded Alfonso's inheritance—an interest in a grand hotel near Sorrento—for a building that had once been Alfonso's grandfather's *pensione* in the village of Sant'Agata sui Due Golfi. At a moment when regional southern cuisine wasn't taken seriously, Alfonso and Livia dreamed of a world-class restaurant that would showcase local ingredients skillfully prepared, elegantly presented, and paired with fine wines. They named their restaurant Don Alfonso, after Alfonso's grandfather. I fell in love with the restaurant and its owners. They showed me their organic vegetable garden, which hugged a cliff overlooking the sea, the groves where they grew olives for their own extra virgin, and the dairy that made their mozzarella and hand-churned butter. They argued about which regional wines they wanted me to taste.

Livia and Alfonso were joined eventually by their sons Ernesto (in the kitchen) and Mario (in the dining room), and Don Alfonso became the first restaurant south of Tuscany to garner well-deserved praise from Italian and international publications. They collected wine, which they stored in an amazing cellar of Etruscan origins with a medieval well at the bottom. Many southern Italian restaurateurs were inspired.

Because customers begged to buy their pasta (a special selection from nearby Gragnano), tomato sauce, and other fine regional products, they opened a shop across from the restaurant with a comfortable cigar lounge, library, and selection of fine distillates sold by the glass or bottle. I can't live without their tomato purée, with intense hyper-tomato flavors.

To represent the Iaccarino family, I at first thought to include the restaurant's vaunted "Vesuvius" timbales of rigatoni, served there with three different sauces—it take two days to prepare and many pages to explain. But at the end of the day I chose a much simpler, homestyle pasta, a dish I enjoyed at a family dinner on the night before Christmas. If you want the more challenging Vesuvius instructions, e-mail me at info@faithwillinger.com.

SPAGHETTI WITH WALNUTS AND ANCHOVIES

FIRST COURSE

SERVES 4 TO 6

¼ cup extra virgin olive oil

3 garlic cloves, sliced

2 whole salt-cured anchovies, filleted, or 4–6 anchovy fillets

3–4 tablespoons coarsely chopped walnuts

Chili pepper to taste

1 tablespoon minced fresh parsley

Coarse sea salt

14–16 ounces spaghetti

Heat the extra virgin in a large skillet and sauté the garlic over low heat until it barely begins to color. Add the anchovy fillets and, with a wooden spoon, mash them until they dissolve into the oil. Add the walnuts, chili pepper, and parsley; stir to combine and remove from heat.

Bring 5 to 6 quarts of water to a rolling boil. Add about 3 tablespoons

(recipe continues)

of sea salt, then add the spaghetti and cook until it offers considerable resistance to the tooth, approximately three-quarters of the package-recommended cooking time. Drain the pasta, reserving 2 cups of the starchy pasta cooking water.

Add the spaghetti to the sauce in the skillet along with ½ cup reserved pasta-cooking water, and cook over high heat, stirring with a wooden fork, until the pasta is cooked al dente, adding a little more pasta water as the sauce dries.

Alfonso and Annamaria Mattozzi

MY FAVORITE RESTAURANT in Naples is L'Europeo, owned by Alfonso Mattozzi. My friends Franco, Antonio, and Carla Sersale introduced me to Alfonso and his wife, Annamaria, and when I tasted their homestyle cooking I knew I'd found a jewel. To this day I never pass through Naples without stopping by for a meal. The decor is typical trattoria: fish tank in the entry, a glass-fronted refrigerator displaying vibrant local produce, and walls covered with paintings and prints of Naples, decorative plates, and large copper pots and molds, all surrounding tables of happy regulars.

Alfonso's powerful sense of hospitality makes everyone who enters feel welcome, as if he or she had arrived at a special destination. As he escorts diners to their tables he informs them of the day's specials. I've never seen anyone with a menu—Alfonso simply explains what's fresh and can't be missed. I always begin with pizza, a taste of classic margherita with tomatoes, mozzarella, and basil, and let Alfonso choose another, like an unforgettable calzone—dough folded over a filling of bitter greens (*friarielli*) and smoked provola cheese, or another with just-born anchovies, *cincinielli* in Neapolitan dialect. It's difficult to resist Alfonso's

L'EUROPEO DI MATTOZZI

Via Campodisola 4/6/8
80133 Napoli
Tel/Fax: +39-081-5521323
Open for lunch Monday–Saturday,
dinner Thursday–Saturday.
Closed Sundays, August 15–31,
and all day Saturday in July.

B&B COSTANTINOPOLI 104

Via S. Maria di Costantinopoli 104
80138 Napoli
Tel: +39-081-557-1035
Fax: +39-081-557-1051

suggestions, but I rarely make it to the main course. And even when I flatly state that dessert is out of the question, somehow it appears nonetheless: traditional Neapolitan desserts like babà or pastiera, along with fresh seasonal fruit that always seem to disappear despite our protests. Alfonso and Annamaria are eager to turn everyone on to the wonders of Naples, dispensing information about their favorite B&B, lesser-known tourist destinations, and shops.

I'm wild about L'Europeo's pasta with mussels. It's made with small, unopened male zucchini flowers, called *sciurilli* in dialect, and finished with Parmigiano, a rule-breaker (serving cheese with fish is generally frowned upon) that works. If you can't find (or harvest) small, green, unopened zucchini flowers, use the freshest squash blossoms you can find. And if you can't find either, you might try the recipe with a couple of thinly sliced zucchini.

PASTA WITH MUSSELS AND ZUCCHINI FLOWERS

FIRST COURSE

SERVES 4 TO 6

¼ cup extra virgin olive oil
4–6 ounces zucchini flowers, preferably closed and green
Fine sea salt and freshly ground black pepper
2 garlic cloves
2 pounds mussels, cleaned
1 tablespoon chopped fresh parsley
14–16 ounces large rigatoni
½ cup grated Parmigiano-Reggiano cheese

In a large skillet, heat 2 tablespoons of the extra virgin over high heat and add the zucchini flowers. Sauté until wilted. Season with salt and pepper, then remove from the skillet.

(recipe continues)

In 4-quart pot, sauté the garlic cloves in the remaining 2 tablespoons extra virgin, and when they begin to brown, add the mussels, cover the pot, and cook over high heat for 3 to 5 minutes or until the mussels open. Sprinkle with the parsley, cover, and set aside.

Bring a large pot with 5 or 6 quarts of water to a rolling boil. Add 2 or 3 tablespoons of salt and the pasta. Cook the pasta until it offers considerable resistance to the tooth, around three-quarters of the package-recommended cooking time.

Using a slotted spoon or skimmer, transfer the mussels to individual serving bowls. Put the pot with the broth on low heat.

Drain the pasta, reserving 1 cup of the pasta water. Transfer the pasta to the pot with the mussel broth, add the zucchini flowers, and ⅓ cup Parmigiano and cook over high heat until the pasta is done. Add the pasta water ¼ cup at a time if the sauce gets too dry. Divide the pasta into the serving bowls and mix with the mussels. Top with the remaining Parmigiano.

Antonietta Gargiulo and Peppe de Simone; Santina Coppola

RISTORANTE LO SCOGLIO is my dream of a fish restaurant, a no-frills kind of place on a dock, overlooking the sea. The most direct route to this restaurant is by water, since there's a landing for boats. The drive by land is a challenge, the road narrow and intestinal in its winding bends. But Lo Scoglio is a grand incentive. Those who drive will find outside the restaurant's entrance a gurgling saltwater tank holding plastic baskets of mollusks. Antonietta, the chef, has a vegetable garden to supplement the bounty of local fishermen, and she presses oil from her own olives. She cooks in an apron-covered housecoat and wears slippers. Her son Peppe de Simone and daughter-in-law Santina Coppola wait on tables, greeting returning clients (even second-timers) like old friends.

LO SCOGLIO

Piazza delle Sirene, 15
Marina del Cantone
80061 Massa Lubrense (NA)
Tel: +39-081-808-1026
Fax: +39-081-808-2870
info@loscoglionerano.com
www.loscoglionerano.com
Open daily; reservations a must.

There are many dishes here that I simply can't resist, beginning with the octopus salad ("fresh local octopus, frozen to tenderize, then boiled, dressed with juice from our lemons, our oil, our parsley"), and a large oval copper pan with tastes of seasonal vegetable dishes, like stuffed chicory, baked peppers, eggplant two different ways, and garlicky zucchini. However, I never dine at Lo Scoglio without a taste of Antonietta's clams. They're the real, true wild *vongole verace* (*Tapes decussatus*), not the farmed Manila clams (*Tapes semidecussatus*) that are sold throughout Italy as *vongole,* and they're truly happy clams, their siphons spitting seawater in Antonietta's tanks. You can attempt the same effect by soaking your clams in a mixture of filtered water and sea salt (the sea substitute, a primal recipe), and if they're lively, they will behave the way they do at Lo Scoglio. Antonietta always asks clients if they want their clams "stained" with tomato, an option I forbear at Lo Scoglio, although at home, without the benefit of superior clams, I stain.

SAUTÉED TRUE CLAMS

SERVES 4

4 cups filtered water
2 tablespoons fine sea salt
2 pounds Manila clams (or cockles, if you can't get them)
3 tablespoons extra virgin olive oil
2 garlic cloves, peeled and lightly mashed
½ cup diced cherry tomatoes (optional)
1 tablespoon minced flat-leaf parsley
Rustic country-style bread

Mix the filtered water and sea salt in a bowl. Pick over the clams and discard those with broken shells and those that are open. Place the clams in the salted water and soak for at least 20 minutes. If your clams are fresh, they'll open up and start spitting, just like Antonietta's.

Lift the clams out of the salted water and put into another bowl, leaving any expelled sand or grit behind. Heat the extra virgin in a large skillet over high heat. Add the garlic, and when it begins to color, add the clams and the optional tomatoes. Cover and cook until the clams open, 3 to 4 minutes.

Transfer clams to a serving dish, top with parsley, and serve with rustic bread to soak up the clam juices.

Berardino Lombardo and Nadia de Simone

I BUMPED INTO Nadia de Simone's husband, Daniele, who used to work in Friuli at Blasut when I was dining at the Oasis (page 228), and he told me that he thought I'd love the restaurant, La Caveja, where his wife was working. He was right. Berardino Lombardo—tall, handsome, bearded, blue-eyed—is the powerhouse behind La Caveja, hidden on a curve before the village of Pietravairano, about an hour south of Rome. There's a casual wine bar, where locals snack on homemade *salumi,* cheese, a few simple dishes, and wine, and La Stalla, a comfortable one-room restaurant housed in the stables, a culinary destination where Nadia de Simone charms. On my first visit Berardino was basting a capon turning on a spit-roaster in the hearth fireplace. I was entranced.

LA CAVEJA

Via Santissima Annunziata 10

81050 Pietravairano (CE)

Tel: +39-0823-984-824

Fax: +39-0823-982-977

albergoristorantecaveja@virgilio.it

All credit cards accepted. Closed Sunday evenings, all day Monday, and December 23–January 8.

Berardino's organic farm supplies the restaurant with poultry, rabbits, pork, *salumi,* and a garden of heirloom vegetables and fruits. The menu is pure tradition, with local just-made mozzarella, sheep's milk ricotta, and polenta sauced with sausage, for starters. Diners continue with soup, then handmade pasta or gnocchi, but there are always two different kinds of *pancotto,* or bread cooked with vegetables. The bread is outstanding, baked in a wood-burning oven. Also look for main courses like simple roast chicken or capon, packed with flavor. There's local pecorino aged in *barrique* casks, caciocavallo cheese aged six, twelve, or eighteen months, jam tarts (with homemade jam from organic heirloom fruit), *conventuali* butter cookies, spiraled with nuts and raisins, and *scauratielli,* or boiled cookies drenched with honey

LA REGGIA: ROYAL PALACE AND PARK OF CASERTA

www.ambientece.arti.beniculturali.it/guida—reggia/Xenglish/index.htm

ENOTECA LA BOTTE

Via Appia, 168
81022 Casagiove (CE)
Tel: +39-0823-494-040
Fax: +39-0823-468-130
info@enotecalabotte.it
www.enotecalabotte.it

CAPUA

Museo Camparo:
www.museocamparo.it

and orange zest. Each course can be paired with an appropriate area wine by the glass or diners can choose from the surprisingly extensive list of Italian wines, especially strong in the wines of Campania.

Simple, reasonably priced rooms upstairs make La Caveja very convenient for touring the area. Visit Caserta, with Europe's largest palace and garden, La Reggia, and the nearby enoteca La Botte, well supplied with a super selection of Italian and regional foods and wines. Or Capua, where the provincial museum has over 150 larger-than-life earth mother fertility goddesses. There are lots of cultural excuses for a stay at La Caveja.

My Tuscan husband adores Berardino's Pancotto, made with turnip greens or with beans. Substitute 2 cups of beans for the cooked greens and add vegetable stock or bean-cooking water (but not the slimy stuff from a can) instead of the water from the greens, and proceed with the recipe as directed.

FIRST COURSE

PANCOTTO

SERVES 4 TO 6

1 pound turnip greens, broccoli rabe, or wild greens
Coarse sea salt
½ cup best-quality extra virgin olive oil
2 garlic cloves, peeled
1 dried chili pepper, cut in half
3–4 cups cubed (½-inch) stale bread (rustic and water based, not fat-enriched)
Fine sea salt

Bring a large pot with at least 4 quarts of water to a rolling boil. While waiting for the water to boil, clean the greens, eliminating tough stems. Add 4 tablespoons coarse sea salt to the boiling water, add the greens, and cook for 5 minutes or until tender; the central leaf rib will be soft when pinched. Drain the greens into a colander, reserving 2 cups of cooking water. Then cool the greens under running cold water, squeeze out excess water, and coarsely chop.

Heat ¼ cup of the extra virgin in a large skillet, add the garlic and chili pepper, and sauté until the garlic begins to brown. Remove the garlic and chili pepper from the oil, add the chopped greens, and sauté so they absorb the oil.

Add the bread cubes and ½ cup reserved cooking water and sauté over high heat so that the bread absorbs the greens, oil, and liquid. Add more reserved cooking water, ½ cup at a time, if necessary to keep mixture moist. Pancotto should be moist but not soupy.

Remove from the heat and add the remaining ¼ cup extra virgin. Taste and add fine sea salt if necessary. Stir and serve.

Tonino and Rita Mellino

I MET TONINO MELLINO in Le Marche when a restaurateur friend offered late one evening to introduce me to a bunch of his restaurateur friends and a winemaker. Through the thickest of fogs we drove on back roads to what he considered a "nearby restaurant"; when we arrived at 11 P.M., they were just beginning their main course. We joined their party; drank some wine; talked about restaurants, food, and cooking techniques; and tasted a strange dessert—homemade panettone with custard sauce (delicious) topped with truffles (not delicious in this context), hanging out until 3 A.M. I promised to visit Tonino at his restaurant, Quattro Passi, the next time I stayed in Positano.

Quattro Passi, as its name declares, is a short walk—only four steps—

QUATTRO PASSI

Via Vespucci, 13/n
80061 Marina del Cantone,
Massalubrense (NA)
Tel: +39-081-808-2800
Tel/Fax: +39-081-808-1271
info@ristorantequattropassi.com
www.ristorantequattropassi.com
Closed Wednesdays; closed Tuesday
evenings October–March; closed
November 4–December 26.
All credit cards accepted.

from the port of Marina del Cantone and the inland village of Nerano on the Amalfi Coast. A yellow minivan ferries diners who arrive by sea; those who drive from Positano, as my husband and I did, cover kilometers of curves. Tonino's wife, Rita, enthusiastically hosts the dining rooms, while he divides his time between the front of the house and the kitchen, executing an ever-changing menu with strictly local ingredients, including just-picked vegetables and super-fresh fish and seafood. Diners at the next table moaned with pleasure when they tasted their lunch. Me, too. Dine on wild carpet-shell and warty Venus clam soup, gently flavored with garlic, tomato, and parsley; sweet-as-sugar langoustines paired with steamed artichokes; fish of the day with black olives, escarole, and capers *in cartoccio,* or cooked in foil. A rustic whole-wheat anise loaf and other, more refined homemade breads are useful for soaking up sauce—acceptable behavior in Italy, especially when the sauce is so delicious. Seasonal sorbetto—lemon, tangerine, prickly pear—are refreshing, but I can't resist the chocolate-glazed half-sphere of barely-held-together chocolate mousse on a slim round slice of cake. Eat on the terrace above the restaurant when the weather is nice and stay in one of Quattro Passi's three comfortable suites so you can dig deeply into the fine wine list and selection of distillates without the need to drive. Purchase a perfect gastronomic souvenir at the enoteca—wine, cheese, pasta (like *paccheri*), or home-cured tuna.

Tonino and Rita gave me a recipe for the most typical of territorial dishes: Paccheri, or wide stubby tubes of pasta, sauced with a fish ragù. If you can't find paccheri, use any short tubular pasta, the bigger the better.

PACCHERI DI GRAGNANO WITH FISH RAGÙ

SERVES 4 TO 6

1 whole fish with head and bones, 1–1½ pounds, the freshest
   possible, firm white flesh
2 garlic cloves
1 chili pepper
¼ cup plus 2 tablespoons extra virgin olive oil
¼ cup dry white wine
½ cup cherry tomatoes, quartered
1 tablespoon minced fresh parsley
Salt
16 ounces paccheri di Gragnano (sometimes called schiaffoni) or
   large rigatoni

Clean, bone, and fillet the fish, saving the bones and head. Chop one garlic glove and the chili pepper together. Heat ¼ cup of the extra virgin in a
skillet and sauté the garlic-chili mixture briefly until it begins to color.
Add the fish head and bones, stir, and after a few minutes add the wine,
tomatoes, 1 cup of water, and the parsley. Lightly season with salt and
simmer for 25 minutes. Strain the sauce and set aside.

Heat the remaining 2 tablespoons extra virgin in a large skillet and
add the other garlic clove, chopped, and the fish fillets, breaking them up
with a wooden fork or spoon, and cook for 5 minutes. Add the strained
sauce and season with salt.

Bring a large pot with 5 quarts of water to a rolling boil; add 3 tablespoons sea salt and the pasta. Cook the pasta until it offers considerable
resistance to the tooth, around three-quarters of the recommended package cooking time. Drain the pasta, reserving 1 cup of the pasta-cooking
water. Add the pasta to the sauce and cook over high heat to amalgamate. Add some of the pasta-cooking water if sauce dries out too much
before the pasta is cooked.

Mario Avallone

A N ENOLOGIST FRIEND claimed that Mario Avallone knew where to find the best pizza in Naples and was about to open a new restaurant, expanding his previous place, a private club in his home with just one table. Of course I was intrigued, and I called to arrange a meeting. Mario picked me up on his motor scooter. I rode helmet-less on the back seat as he wove through Neapolitan traffic, which is scary enough in a car (traffic lights in this city are a mere suggestion). My husband told

LA STANZA DEL GUSTO

Vicoletto Sant'Arpino, 21
80100 Napoli
Tel: +39-081-401-578
Closed Sundays and Mondays;
closed 3 weeks in August.

PEPE BROTHERS

Vico della Graziella, 17
80100 Napoli
Tel: +39-081-551-0116
Custom copper, tin, iron, and
brass work.

UNIVERSITA' DI STRADA, RICCARDO DALISI SCULPTURE

Rua Catalana, 11
80100 Napoli
Tel: +39-081-551-0116

PERXICHELLA

Via Pallonetto a S. Chiara, 36
80100 Napoli
Tel: +39-081-551-0025

me I was crazy, and he was right, but it was worth the terrifying ride. We visited the Pepe brothers—tin artisans who took us to the studio of Ricardo Dalisi, which was filled with sculptures including an elaborate Christmas crèche and a series of pieces made of Neapolitan *caffettiere,* part of a project he designed for Alessi. Next we stopped at Mario's favorite chocolate shop, Perxichella, where the chocolate is crafted by hand. I couldn't resist a chocolate mask of Toto', legendary Neapolitan comic. We had lunch at a seedy but fantastic pizzeria in the infamous Salute neighborhood, then moved on to an outdoor market, where of course Mario knew which vendors had the best stuff. We snacked on sfogliatelle pastries, both preferring *riccia,* the crispy version, then scootered back to his restaurant, La Stanza del Gusto, hidden at the end of a quiet lane in the heart of Naples, with a sign out front made by the Pepe brothers.

The decor at La Stanza del Gusto is sunny and Mediterranean, with walls painted in wide stripes of saffron and spinach green and a large round table in the center of the dining room proudly displaying a big papier-mâché pig centerpiece. Mario's cooking is Neapolitan, but it is influenced by a ten-year stay in Sicily and inspired by the daily market. Order by the course or tasting menu—three or five courses, paired with appropriate wines. Mario is wild about cheese, and ages cheese he gets from a network of fine artisanal makers in a cellar next to the restaurant. Cheese lovers should plan a pilgrimage. The wine selection is as interesting, as personal as the rest of the experience.

Mario's cold pasta salad uses seasonal beans called *spollechini* in the regional dialect, or fresh tender white beans in a pod. If you can't find fresh beans in pods, substitute fresh lima beans, cook up some dried white beans, or use canned beans if you're really in a hurry.

PIZZERIA ADDÒ RICCIO

Via Fontanelle 46/47

Capodimonte

80100 Napoli

Tel: +39-081-544-6292

SFOGLIATELLE ATTANASIO

Vico Ferrovia, 2/3/4

80100 Napoli

Closed Mondays.

PASTA AND BEAN SALAD WITH CELERY PESTO

SERVES 8 TO 10

3 pounds fresh beans in pods, or 4 cups cooked beans
1–3 garlic cloves
1 medium bunch celery, with leaves if possible
Sea salt
10–12 ounces short, small pasta or broken spaghetti
½ cup extra virgin olive oil
Freshly ground black pepper

If you're lucky enough to get fresh beans, shell them, put them in a pot with 8 cups water, a garlic clove, and a tough outer celery stalk and cook until the beans are tender. Or begin with 4 cups of cooked beans. Drain the beans.

Bring 5 quarts of water to a rolling boil, add 2 to 3 tablespoons of salt and the pasta, and cook until al dente. Drain the pasta (but don't throw the water away—you'll use it to make the celery pesto) and put it in a colander with ice cubes, chilling the pasta and melting the cubes. Transfer the chilled pasta to a bowl, combine with the beans, toss with 3 tablespoons extra virgin, and season with salt and pepper.

Remove any remaining outer tough stalks of the celery and cut the central part into 1-inch pieces. Cook the celery in the pasta-cooking water for 5 minutes, drain, and chill in a colander with ice cubes.

Purée the celery (and some of the leaves, uncooked, if you have them) with 2 garlic cloves and 3 tablespoons extra virgin in a blender or with an immersion mixer, then season well with salt and pepper. Add to the beans and pasta.

Thinly slice one celery stalk (and some celery leaves if you have them) and use to garnish the pasta and bean salad. Finish each bowl with a generous drizzle of extra virgin.

Elio, Francesco, and Marina Mariani

CHECCHINO HAS ALWAYS been one of Rome's best restaurants. Located in the area known as Testaccio, it serves traditional dishes cooked to perfection, paired with wines from one of the city's best wine cellars. The Mariani family's restaurant began life in 1887 as a shop that sold wine to workers at the slaughterhouse across the street; a few years later it evolved into an osteria with food. The location gave them access to the best meat in the city, including the "fifth quarter" (left over after the official four quarters) cuts of beef and veal, such as the head, tail, hoof, innards, and tripe that are used in traditional Roman dishes. A wine cellar was carved from the ancient Roman landfill of Testaccio (from *testa, testae,* Latin for "wine amphora"), revealing bits and pieces of broken amphora and pottery, which help insulate the cellar.

CHECCHINO
DAL 1887

Osteria Romana
Via di Monte Testaccio, 30
00153 Roma
Tel: +39-06-574-3816
Fax: +39-06-574-6318
checchino_roma@tin.it
www.checchino-dal-1887.com
Closed Sundays and Mondays,
all of August, and
December 24–January 2.
All credit cards accepted.

The fifth generation of Marianis—brothers (and sommeliers) Elio and Francesco and their sister Marina—now run Checchino, and it's better than ever. They've filled the cellar with an amazing collection of wines, and they still serve the same food that put this classic restaurant on the culinary map: *testina* (veal-head terrine); pastas like *amatriciana, carbonara,* and *gricia* made with *guanciale* (cured pork jowl); tonarelli pasta with oxtail sauce; fifth-quarter preparations like *pajata* (milk-fed veal intestine), as well as Roman vegetable dishes like artichokes, fava beans, Catalan chicory, and broccoli.

When I was writing *Red, White & Greens,* about Italian vegetables, I asked Elio and Francesco if I could observe in their kitchen. After a whole morning in which I learned to clean artichokes like a pro (the first 300 are the hardest!), scribbling notes all the while, they asked me to have lunch with the family. We ate Bucatini alla Gricia, or long slender tubes of pasta that are one of the more challenging shapes to twirl—think garden hose on a fork. I needed the recipe because it's made with ingredients that are always on hand in my kitchen. Rigatoni or even spaghetti can be substituted for bucatini, but don't use bacon or any smoky pork product because "it will unbalance the dish," warn the Mariani brothers.

FIRST COURSE

BUCATINI ALLA GRICIA

SERVES 4 TO 6

2–3 tablespoons coarse sea salt
14–16 ounces pasta, preferably bucatini
4½ ounces salt-and-pepper-cured pork jowl, or salt pork
      or any fatty cured (but not smoked) pork like pancetta,
      sliced ¼ inch thick
⅔ cup grated pecorino romano cheese (aged if possible)
1 teaspoon freshly ground black pepper

Bring 6 quarts of water to a rolling boil; add the salt and the pasta. Cook the pasta until it offers some resistance to the tooth, a little more than three-quarters of the recommended cooking time. Drain, reserving 2 or 3 cups of pasta-cooking water.

While the pasta is cooking, dice the pork and cook over medium-high heat in a large skillet (cast iron, if you want to be traditional) until browned and crisp. If the pork is too lean and no fat is rendered, you may need to add a tablespoon of extra virgin to help the process.

Add the pasta to the skillet and add half the grated cheese, the pepper, and ¾ cup of the pasta-cooking water. Cook over the highest heat until the pasta is al dente, 3 or 4 minutes. Add more pasta-cooking water if the sauce is too dry. Serve in warm bowls, topped with the remaining grated cheese.

Paola and Armando di Mauro

N ASSIGNMENT to write about Roman food and wine for a shopping guide gave me an opportunity to approach Paola di Mauro, owner of Lazio's most interesting winery, Colle Picchioni, and the goddess of Roman cooking. She agreed to be interviewed and picked me up at the Cinecittá bus stop to shop for our lunch's ingredients in the villages of the Castelli Romani. Paola talked food a mile a minute and with a serious Roman accent, punctuating her discussion of groceries and what she planned to do with them with gossip about restaurants, chefs, and winemakers.

We went to a *forno* bakery in Grottaferrata for bread. "Wood-burning oven, open seven days a week," explained Paola as she purchased a huge dark, round loaf and a chunk of the olive oil–glazed flatbread called pizza bianca to snack on. At the butcher's I got an anatomy lesson as Paola showed me calf's sweetbreads, glands, and intestines and pointed out all the components of *coratella*: lamb's liver, lungs, heart, and spleen. She purchased some thick-sliced calf's liver to bake with potatoes, bread crumbs, garlic, and extra virgin and some just-made sheep's milk ricotta and a hunk of pecorino romano from a nearby dairy. The garden beyond her dining room door provided most of the produce. Paola pointed out *rughetta,* or wild arugula: "Look at the leaves—they're different from the cultivated kind." And there was *mentuccia,* or Roman mint, and ripe apricots on her trees. Wine, of course, came from the vineyards outside her front door—a simple red, DOC whites Marino and Marino Selezione Oro, and an important red, Vigna del Vasallo.

I helped Paola unload the groceries, then she tied on an apron and, with no apparent rush, prepared an eight-course lunch. My notes and recipes were peppered with Paola's Roman narrative. I've since seen Paola cook lunch and dinner many times for visiting restaurateurs, jour-

COLLE PICCHIONI

Via di Colle Picchione, 46

00040 Frattocchie, Marino (RM)

Tel: +39-06-935-46329

Fax: +39-06-935-48440

info@collepicchioni.it

www.collepicchioni.it

Visits by appointment only.

nalists, politicians, friends, and family, but my favorite recipe, the one I make all the time, is one she made for dinner for just the two of us: Potato and Pasta Soup. The pasta absorbs a great deal of the water, and it's flavored with garlic, black pepper, quality extra virgin, and grated Parmigiano-Reggiano. It doesn't look like much until it's almost cooked, then it's simply delicious.

FIRST COURSE   ## PAOLA'S POTATO AND PASTA SOUP

SERVES 1 TO 2

¾ cup peeled and diced potato
Sea salt
1 ounce finest quality spaghetti, broken into 1-inch pieces
1 garlic clove, peeled
1 teaspoon black peppercorns
2 tablespoons extra virgin olive oil
2–3 tablespoons grated Parmigiano-Reggiano cheese

Put 2 cups of water, the potato, and salt to taste in a saucepan. Bring to a boil and simmer for 5 to 8 minutes or until the potato is almost cooked. Add the broken pasta and simmer for 10 minutes more.

While the pasta is cooking, mash the garlic in a mortar, then add the pepper and crush coarsely. Add to the soup and continue cooking until the pasta is cooked al dente. Ladle the soup into a bowl, and top with a drizzle of extra virgin and the Parmigiano-Reggiano.

*   *   *

Antonella Ricci and Vinod Sookar; Rosella Ricci and Tomaso Gioia

AL FORNELLO DA RICCI

Contrada Montevicoli, 71
72013 Ceglie Messapica (BR)
Tel/Fax: +39-0831-377-104
ricciristor@libero.it
www.jre.it/italiano/b/
ristoratore.xtmlid=10.html
www.mangiarebene.net/
CHEFS/ricci
Closed Monday evenings and all
day Tuesday, plus February and
September. All credit cards
accepted.

THE RICCI SISTERS literally grew up at Al Fornello da Ricci— Antonella in the kitchen, sommelier Rosella in the dining room. Their input at their parents' restaurant is so evident, so different, in part due to the influence of Antonella's husband/chef, Vinod Sookar. The couple met in Mauritius, where she cooked a series of dinners promoting the region of Puglia and he was a young local chef in the kitchen. They fell in love and Vinod moved to Ceglie to work in the family restaurant. Antonella joined a young chef's organization and together she and Vinod introduced several less traditional dishes to the menu. Their cucina, however, is still based on superb local ingredients.

Like her sister, Rosella grew up in the restaurant and helped when a hand was needed on weekends and holidays. Her real interest, though, was music; she studied, then taught at a local music academy until her father's passion for wine caught up with her. Rosella now teaches part time and shares sommelier duties with Angelo at the restaurant. Both believe strongly in the power of the native Pugliese grape varietals, like negro amaro, uva di troia, and primitivo, but Rosella appreciates the addition of cabernet and merlot wines for an international palate. Rosella's husband, Tomaso, works behind the scenes, dealing with Italian restaurant bureaucracy and accounting.

This recipe is a perfect example of Antonella and Vinod's new take on an old dish; gnocchi without the heaviness of eggs and flour in the dough. Dress their gnocchi with butter (or extra virgin) and grated pecorino, or with a simple tomato sauce and grated pecorino. Rosella suggests serving them with a glass of dry white wine, like Briciole, Masseria Monaci's Salento IGT.

RICOTTA GNOCCHI

SERVES 4 TO 6

1 cup drained ricotta, preferably local, or sheep's milk
½ cup grated dry pecorino, preferably imported romano, cheese
Freshly ground black pepper
4 cups durum wheat flour (semolina)
Sea salt
3 tablespoons unsalted butter, melted, or extra virgin olive oil
  (or tomato sauce)

Combine the ricotta, 2 to 3 tablespoons of the pecorino, and pepper in a food processor. Process until the mixture is smooth and well combined. (Or beat with a hand mixer until the same effect is achieved.)

Put half the flour in a 10 by 15-inch cookie sheet with edges.

Put the ricotta mixture in a pastry bag and pipe rounded teaspoonfuls onto the flour. (Or, using 2 teaspoons, form the gnocchi and drop onto the flour.) Cover the gnocchi with the remaining flour and refrigerate for at least 24 hours or up to two days.

Bring 4 to 5 quarts of water to a rolling boil in a large pot. Add 3 tablespoons salt.

Remove the gnocchi from the flour and dust lightly to remove excess. (Note: flour can be sifted to remove any ricotta, then frozen for future use making these gnocchi.)

Poach the gnocchi, around eight at a time, for 3 minutes after they float to the surface—they may need a little coaxing with a slotted spoon. Remove to a warm serving dish, drizzle with the melted butter (or extra virgin) or warm tomato sauce, if you prefer, and top with the remaining pecorino.

*   *   *

Camillo, Roberta, Simona, and Giuseppe Guerra

*N*AMED FOR a large pomegranate tree (*melograno*) that grows in its courtyard, Il Melograno in Monopoli, Puglia was the first *masseria* farmhouse in the area to be converted into an elegant hotel. Owner Camillo Guerra was in the antique business, and he and his family restored and furnished the farm and outbuildings with style, filling them with antiques and building around the ancient olive tree with its gnarled trunks, and planting a citrus grove near the outdoor swimming pool. His respect for the region extends to the restaurant, which serves fantastic traditional dishes made from local, seasonal ingredients—expect lots of interesting vegetable preparations, homemade pasta like cavatelli and orecchiette, amazing fresh cheeses like mozzarella, ricotta, and burrata. Camillo's daughter Roberta helps run the hotel, assisted by her sister Simona and their brother Giuseppe, who manages La Peschiera beach club, a perfect spot for spending a day at the beach, with its spring-fed saltwater pool, bar, and seafood restaurant. One visit was enough to fall in love with Il Melograno, and I vowed to return because Camillo, a discriminating diner, had promised to make me *tianedde,* a traditional dish that's usually made for a crowd and rarely found in restaurants.

He made good on that promise when I visited with a group of food-writer friends, and we observed Camillo in the kitchen, with Roberta supervising the preparation of the *tianedde.* Mussels were split, vegetables were prepped, Camillo scattered the ingredients in layers in a terra-cotta pot called a *tianedde* in regional dialect. While the dish baked in the oven, Roberta and Camillo discussed the ingredients—wild arugula, local extra virgin, bread from a wood-burning oven, hand-formed pasta made with local hard wheat, dairy products like burrata, mozzarella, and fresh,

IL MELOGRANO

Contrada Torricella, 345 (SW)
70043 Monopoli (BA)
Tel: +39-080-690-9030
Fax: +39-080-747-908
melograno@melograno.com
www.melograno.com
Closed February.
All credit cards accepted.

salted, or "strong" ricotta—that are all essential elements of their regional cuisine. Later we adjourned to the table and feasted on the *tianedde*. I returned home with lots of notes and a terra-cotta *tianedde* (although a paella pan will do for those who don't have a *tianedde* of their own). In reproducing Camillo's recipe, I steamed the mussels open and saved the broth, which is much less work than prying the mussels open, but those who wish to pry instead should feel free to do so.

FIRST COURSE

BAKED RICE, POTATO, AND MUSSEL TIANEDDE

SERVES 6 TO 8

¾ cup plus 2 tablespoons Carnaroli or Arborio rice

2½ pounds mussels

3 tablespoons fresh flat-leaf parsley

2–3 garlic cloves

½ cup extra virgin olive oil

1 large onion, cut in half and thinly sliced

1½–1¾ pounds potatoes, peeled and sliced ¼ inch thick

1 cup diced fresh or canned tomato

Sea salt and freshly ground black pepper

¾ cup grated pecorino cheese

Put the rice in 2 cups of cold water while you're cleaning the mussels.

Clean the mussels, removing the beards and scrubbing under cold water. Either pry open the mussels or steam them until barely opened and cool. Remove one shell, leaving the mussel in the other half. If you've steamed the mussels, strain and reserve the liquid.

Preheat the oven to 375°F.

Mince the parsley and garlic together.

Drain the rice but reserve the starchy water.

Drizzle a teaspoon of extra virgin on the bottom of a 12-inch heavy-bottomed flameproof casserole, paella pan, or terra-cotta pan (for traditionalists like Camillo), and scatter some onion slices on the oil. Top with a layer of potato, scatter with 3 tablespoons tomato, then some of the parsley-garlic mix, salt, and pepper. Cover with a layer of mussels on the half-shell, then scatter with ¼ cup soaked rice. Sprinkle with the pecorino, drizzle with oil, and season with salt and pepper. Make another layer of onion, potato, tomato, parsley-garlic, salt and pepper, mussels, rice, and pecorino, then make another layer. Top with remaining rice, then potato, tomato, and pecorino. Drizzle with oil, season with salt and pepper.

In a saucepan, bring the starchy water and the mussel liquid (if you steamed the mussels) to a boil. Add to the casserole, and then add boiling water until it reaches just below the top layer. Bring to a simmer over medium-high heat (on a flame-tamer if you're using terra cotta; this will take a while), then transfer to the oven and bake for 40 to 45 minutes. Remove from oven and let rest for 10 minutes before serving.

Peppe Zullo

I WAS ON MY WAY home from the Gargano area of northern Puglia when a friend suggested that I spend the night in the village of Orsara di Puglia, where restaurateur Peppe Zullo had just about completed five suites in a building behind his eponymous restaurant. I arrived not really hungry after an overenthusiastic lunch in Foggia, but my appetite picked up when I smelled meat roasting in the wood-burning oven and noticed a large basket of wild greens and herbs and another basket filled with *mele limoncelle*—small, yellow, almost-oval-shaped wild apples—on a stainless-steel counter in the kitchen. Peppe spoke to me in English and explained that he'd cooked in Boston for a few years, then moved to Mexico, where he opened his own restaurant in Puerta Vallarta before moving back to his home town of Orsara when his Mexican marriage fell apart. Everyone in the village calls him *Il Messicano.*

RISTORANTE PEPPE ZULLO

Località Piano Paradiso

71100 Orsara di Puglia (FO)

Tel: +39-0881-964-763

Fax: +39-0881-968-234

info@peppezullo.it

www.peppezullo.it

Closed all November.

Peppe's inn address is appropriate, Piano Paradiso, because he has created his own paradise, with vineyards of local Tuccanese grapes, a small wine cellar next to the restaurant, and winemaking facilities with paintings on the wall by his friend *Il Maestro,* a school chum who's now a famous artist. Dinner was handmade orecchiette and cavatelli sauced with wild greens and herbs; roast kid; tiny, almost-sweet, yellow-fleshed potatoes; and those wild apples glazed with honey and baked in the oven after the meat. We toured the wine cellar and admired the Maestro's paintings before retiring to our rooms. My just-completed suite was a pleasant shock, with a red leather Le Corbusier sofa in the living room. Peppe's got big plans for Orsara, and is restoring a villa that will have

a teaching kitchen, more luxury accommodations, and a conference center. I can't wait for my next visit. I console myself with Peppe's Fava Beans and Chicory or Greens, easier than any version of the soup I've previously prepared. When chicory isn't available, substitute dandelion greens or other fresh leafy greens. I like to garnish the soup with bread crumbs toasted in extra virgin (made from totally stale, dried-out bread) to add a little crunch. If you can't find skinless dried fava beans, you'll have to soak whole ones for 12 hours, then rub them to remove the skins; augment the cooking time depending on the condition of the beans.

SERVES 4 TO 6

2 cups split dried fava beans, without skins

1–1½ pounds chicory, wild greens, broccoli rabe, or spinach

Sea salt

¼ cup extra virgin olive oil, plus more for serving

Freshly ground black pepper

½ cup good quality bread crumbs, toasted in 1 tablespoon
   extra virgin olive oil (optional)

Rinse the split fava beans and soak them in a large bowl of water for 12 hours. Drain the favas, put them in a 4-quart pot, and add fresh water to cover by 2 inches. Bring the water to a boil, lower the heat, and simmer, uncovered, for around 2 hours.

Clean the greens in a sinkful of warm water, trimming off bruised leaves or tough stems. Separate the tougher, outer chicory leaves; break remaining ones into bite-size pieces and split the central part of the chicory into halves or quarters, or chop the greens into bite-size pieces.

When the favas start to break up (after about 2 hours), stir with a wooden spoon until the soup has thickened but the favas aren't totally puréed; the soup should have the texture of porridge. Season with sea salt, then stir in the extra virgin and keep the soup warm.

Bring a large pot with 5 quarts of water to a rolling boil. Add 2 table-spoons sea salt and the greens, adding the tougher outer leaves first. Cook until tender; the time will vary depending on the kind of greens you are using. Remove the greens with a slotted spoon (refresh in cold water if you're preparing the greens in advance and reheat them in the cooking water before serving), and squeeze out the excess water. Ladle the fava bean purée into bowls, top with the greens, then drizzle with some extra virgin, freshly ground black pepper, and bread crumbs if using.

Anna, Costanza, Rosemary, Lucio, Giuseppe, Alberto, and Franca Tasca; Venceslao Lanza

TENUTA DI REGALEALI

Contrada Regaleali
90020 Sclafani Bagni (PA)
Tel: +39-0921-544-011
Fax: +39-0921-542-783
welcome@tascadalmerita.it
www.tascadalmerita.it
Visits by appointment only.

)'D BEEN INVITED for lunch at Regaleali, a Sicilian winery estate owned by the noble Tasca d'Almerita family, and all the official greeters—Count Giuseppe (who traveled with his personal chef), his son Lucio, and even the winemaker were out of town, so Marchesa Anna, the eldest daughter, was my hostess. We had a simple country lunch in her brother's maid's kitchen; the chef was with the count and little attention was paid to wine. Anna told me she'd been thinking about opening a cooking school. I asked why Americans would come all the way to her winery, over an hour from Palermo, based on my lunch. She made me

promise to return so she could show me what was so special about the food and wines of Regaleali.

I did return, and I have been back often since. Eventually I met the whole family: Count Giuseppe, Countess Franca, their son Lucio (and his sons Giuseppe and Alberto), their daughters Costanza and Rosemary (both had married princes), and Anna's husband, Venceslao (he's a marquis). The count and countess lived in Casavecchia, the "Old House," and their children each had restored a farmhouse on the estate. Much of what we ate at Regaleali came from the estate itself. Bread made from local hard wheat is kneaded by hand and baked in a wood-burning oven. Sheep grazed in the fields, and we ate lamb and just-made, still-warm sheep's milk ricotta and fresh tuma cheese. A large garden provided produce, including uncommon Sicilian vegetables and fruits. I have dined in both the banquet hall and the family dining room in the "Old House," feasting on the cooking of the Mario Lo Menzo, one of the last *monzù,* as Sicilian chefs employed by nobles were called. I have also eaten the simpler cooking of Anna, Costanza, and Rosemary in their homes. And of course I have tasted the wines. I was impressed by the easy, everyday qualities of the simpler wines. Special wines—Rosso del Conte and Nozze d'Oro—had great finesse. These were enological whims of the count, who wanted an elegant Sicilian red wine made with Sicilian varietal grapes and a white wine to honor his golden wedding anniversary.

Anna built her cooking school in 1989. In the early years, Mario taught noble Sicilian dishes with Anna translating, but it soon became clear that her students were far more interested in Anna's everyday cooking—and no translations were necessary. Anna also became an author, writing about the foods and wines of Sicily in *The Heart of Sicily, The Flavors of Sicily,* and her self-published *Herbs and Wild Greens from the Sicilian Countryside* and *The Garden of Endangered Fruit.*

We've traveled together, exploring the foods and wines of Sicily, visiting the Aeolian Islands, and the Baroque jewel of Modica, and spending a few weeks cooking together on the island of Pantelleria. I always come home with a suitcase full of food—wild oregano, capers, almonds, pistachio nuts, chocolate, sun-dried tomato paste—and recipes that take me back to Sicily. If you can't visit Sicily and Anna's fantastic cooking school, try this recipe and serve it with one of Regaleali's fine wines.

FIRST COURSE

RISOTTO WITH ALMONDS AND BROCCOLI

SERVES 4 TO 6

1 tablespoon coarse sea salt
1½ cups chopped broccoli, washed and trimmed,
    in bite-size pieces
5–6 cups chicken or vegetable broth or water
1 medium onion, finely chopped
1 garlic clove, finely chopped
3 tablespoons unsalted butter
3 tablespoons extra virgin olive oil
1¼ cups Carnaroli or Vialone Nano rice
¼ cup dry white wine
¼ cup grated Parmigiano-Reggiano cheese
½ cup toasted almonds, roughly chopped

Bring 4 quarts of water to a boil, add the salt, and blanch the broccoli for 4 to 5 minutes or until just tender. Refresh in cold water, drain, and set aside.

Put the broth in a saucepan and bring to a simmer. (If using water, add additional salt.)

In a 4-quart, heavy-bottomed pot, sauté the onion and garlic in 1 tablespoon of the butter and the olive oil over low heat until the onion is transparent. Add the rice, stirring well to coat with oil. Add the wine, turn the heat to high, and cook until the wine evaporates.

Add half the broccoli and a ladleful of the simmering broth, and cook. Stir almost constantly for 15 to 18 minutes, preferably with a long-handled wooden spoon to avoid burns. Continue adding broth whenever the mixture is dry. When done, the rice should be slightly al dente and slightly soupy. Remove from the heat and add the remaining broccoli, remaining 2 tablespoons butter, the Parmigiano-Reggiano, and half the almonds. Cover and let the risotto rest for 3 minutes. Serve garnished with the remaining almonds.

Salvo Stampisi

CATANIA HAS SOME of Italy's most exciting outdoor markets. The Pescheria fish market, in the center of Catania, around the corner from the Duomo, is my favorite. Here, under huge umbrellas or ancient arcades, the bounty of the Sicilian seas is on display: swordfish with swords, crates of silvery-blue anchovies, shrimp with tiny turquoise eggs, gleaming whole fish curved with rigor mortis (a sign of freshness), tubs of gelatinous gray larval fish called "sea foam." The market sprawls into adjacent piazzas and lanes like an Arabian souk with produce and dry goods. A rival market has more stands, more produce, more shops nearby offering bread and refrigerated goods, but the fish selection isn't as vibrant and the tuna is displayed under big red umbrellas that make it look far better than it actually is—an unreal crimson color in all the pictures I took. Nor does the neighborhood offer any potential dining spots.

A friend in the wine business steered me to Antica Marina, right in the Pescheria's piazza; and after watching waiters from the restaurant travel back and forth from what appeared to be the best fish vendor in the market, I decided to try it. Antica Marina's decor is typically Sicilian, with

OSTERIA ANTICA MARINA

Via Pardo, 29
95124 Catania (CT)
Tel/Fax: +39-095-348-197
anticamarina@cataniaatavola.it
www.anticamarina.it
Closed Wednesdays. All credit cards accepted.

decorative plates, cavalier marionettes, miniature carts and horses, and paintings of local scenes. A serious scale (fish is sold by weight) has a place of honor, next to the antipasto display of marinated fish and vegetable salads. The menu features fresh fish, of course, and many of the listings include the words "live" and "local." If you're lucky, as I was, Salvo Stampisi will direct you to the catch of the day, the most interesting preparations. Classic sardine or swordfish rolls, spaghetti with anchovies and bread crumbs, linguini with tuna roe, and deep-fried squidlets in a size defined as "bait" on the menu were all delicious and perfectly executed, but the pasta with shrimp, almonds, and mint was something I wanted to take home as a souvenir of my visit to Catania.

FIRST COURSE

SHORT PASTA WITH SHRIMP AND SICILIAN PESTO

SERVES 6

1 pound large shrimp, with shells
4–6 cherry tomatoes
Salt
2 tablespoons chopped almonds
2 tablespoons pine nuts
1 teaspoon chopped fresh mint
2 tablespoons chopped fresh basil
1 garlic clove
14–16 ounces short pasta

Peel and clean the shrimp. Combine the shrimp shells, tomatoes, and 2 cups water in a large saucepan. Simmer for 30 minutes, then strain the mixture, and reduce the broth over high heat to obtain ¾ cup stock. Adjust for salt.

Combine the almonds, pine nuts, mint, basil, garlic, and ¼ cup of the stock in a blender or purée with an immersion mixer.

Bring a pot with 5 to 6 quarts of water to a rolling boil. Add 2 to 3 tablespoons of salt and the pasta. Cook the pasta until it offers considerable resistance to the tooth, around three-quarters of the package-recommended cooking time. Drain the pasta, reserving 1 cup of the pasta water.

Transfer the pasta to a large skillet or a 3- to 4-quart pot. Add the pesto, ¼ cup stock, and the shrimp. Cook over high heat, stirring gently and frequently, until the pasta is cooked through and the shrimp are hot. Add the pasta water, ¼ cup at a time, if the sauce seems dry.

Salvatore de Gennaro and Anna Maria Cuomo

THE SIGN, written in big red letters on a fence on the road from Naples to Sorrento, was intriguing: *La Tradizione* (the tradition). I simply had to stop. La Tradizione was a *gastronomia*, or grocery store, and the owners were clearly obsessed with tradition and quality. Salvatore de Gennaro's family raised pigs and made *salumi*; Anna Maria Cuomo's family made cheese; and their marriage has resulted in a culinary experience that's worth a voyage. They sell the finest limited-production cheeses, like provolone del Monaco, and pecorino from the rare Laticauda sheep's milk, both aged in grottoes; just-made mozzarella and smoky pro-vola; and tiny baskets of ricotta. *Salumi* are homemade from pork raised by Salvatore's father. Pork cracklings (*ciccioli*), homemade *salumi* like *salame di Sorrento,* and *guanciale* (cured pork jowl) as well as fresh poultry, pork, and lamb are available along with Anna Maria's ready-to-cook dishes like *spiedini* skewers of meat and vegetables and breaded "cutlets" of smoked provola cheese. Products like *taralli* (lard, almond, and black pepper rings); regional pasta shapes like *candele, millerighe,* and *paccheri,* from the nearby village of Gragnano (famous for pasta); extra virgin olive oil; or regional honey are easier-to-handle culinary souvenirs. There's also an ample selection of Campanian, as well as outer-regional wines and spirits.

Anna Maria often prepares a plate of *salumi* or cheese for tasting, and soon everyone in the shop is munching, with Salvatore explaining what, where, how, why. It's always something delicious. Salvatore knows about up-and-coming regional restaurants since he supplies them with cheese and *salumi,* and he travels all over southern Italy, searching for artisanal products at the source. I take notes. Anna Maria uses yesterday's smoked provola for her "cutlets," a dish she always ate at home, since her family had to do something with their day-old cheese, as the locals will only eat it fresh. Since you won't have yesterday's smoked provola, use smoked mozzarella, which is widely available.

LA TRADIZIONE

Via R. Bosco, 969

80069 Seiano di Vico Equense (NA)

Tel: +39-081-802-8869

Fax: +39-081-802-9914

www.latradizione.com

MAIN COURSE

SMOKED MOZZARELLA CUTLETS

SERVES 2

3 eggs

1½–2 cups dried bread crumbs

½ pound smoked mozzarella, sliced ½ inch thick

1½ cups extra virgin olive oil

Beat the eggs with 2 tablespoons water until well combined on a plate. Put the bread crumbs on a flat dinner plate. Dip the mozzarella into the beaten egg, letting the excess egg drip off. Dredge each side in the bread crumbs, and then shake to remove excess. Then re-dip slices into the egg, coating both sides, letting excess egg drip off. Then dredge in bread crumbs again, pressing on both sides so that the cheese is enclosed in an even layer of breading, which will seal in the cheese when it's fried. Chill, covered with a paper towel or cloth, for at least 30 minutes.

Heat the extra virgin in an 8-inch saucepan until hot, 365°F. for those who measure. Fry two slices at a time until the bread crumbs are brown. Drain on paper towels, and serve immediately.

Franco Recati

I WENT TO the village of Barletta, on the coast of Puglia, with Jenn (my indispensable assistant), Josh (her brother, the chef), and Suzanne (my sister, the artist). To work up an appetite before stopping for lunch, we visited the Duomo, a Norman castle and art gallery with a fantastic exhibit of the work of Impressionist Giuseppe de Nittis, then headed for BaccOsteria. I knew Franco Recati from his first restaurant in Barletta, where he earned two Michelin stars serving elegant regional cuisine with exceptional wines. He was lured to Rome, then to the United States, but he's back home at the helm of a casual fish restaurant.

We peered through the thick glass floor of

BACCOSTERIA

Via San Giorgio, 5

70051 Barletta (BA)

Tel: +39-0883-534-000

Fax: +39-0883-533-100

Closed Sunday dinner and all day

Monday; closed August 1–20.

All credit cards accepted.

the main dining room at the cellar, stacked with wooden cases of important, mostly Italian wines, a sign of Franco's ongoing obsession with wine. We let him select an all-seafood menu, but I had to begin with the locally produced burrata, a hollowed-out cow's milk mozzarella that encloses a filling of heavy cream and mozzarella threads. It's one of the most sensual and evanescent cheeses in the world, and Franco's artisanal source didn't disappoint. His superior sourcing continued with the fish and seafood, all local, all super-fresh. We feasted next on a selection of raw fish and seafood: sweet langoustines, tiny wild clams, and razor clams so fresh that one on Jenn's plate tried to escape from her fork, leaping toward Josh, who downed it with no regrets. Spaghetti with sea urchin roe was stellar, but not the kind of recipe I could repeat at home, so Franco gave me the recipe for our main course—fish baked with potatoes. Use the freshest fish you can get your hands on.

MAIN COURSE

BAKED FISH AND POTATOES

SERVES 4 TO 6

¼ cup lightly packed fresh parsley

3 garlic cloves

Fine sea salt

Freshly ground black pepper

¼ cup extra virgin olive oil

1½ pounds potatoes, peeled and thinly sliced

¾ cup cherry tomatoes, cut in half

4 large, firm white fish fillets, 6–8 ounces each
    and around 1 inch thick

¼ cup grated pecorino (Romano is probably the best choice)

Preheat the oven to 475°F.

Mince or process the parsley, garlic, 1 teaspoon salt, and pepper to taste. Set aside.

Drizzle 1 tablespoon extra virgin in a baking dish large enough to hold the fish in one layer. Cover the bottom of the dish with a layer of potatoes, overlapping them to completely cover the pan, and lightly season with salt and pepper. Sprinkle half the parsley-garlic mixture over the potatoes and scatter half the tomatoes over the herbs.

Place the fish fillets in the baking dish on top of the potatoes. Scatter with remaining tomatoes and remaining potato slices. Top the potatoes with grated pecorino and the rest of the parsley mixture. Drizzle with 3 tablespoons extra virgin.

Bake for 25 to 35 minutes. This is a very forgiving recipe; when the potatoes are done, the fish will be, too.

Gegé and Ninni Mangano

I VISITED THE GARGANO area of northern Puglia to write about the restaurant scene in San Giovanni Rotondo, site of the inspired Renzo Piano sanctuary for Saint Pius (formerly and mostly known in Italy as Padre Pio, a favorite of many Italians). The town was bizarre—it's visited by over 8 million pilgrims yearly, and boasts hundreds of new hotel rooms, a huge hospital, endless religious souvenir stands, and a drive-thru McDonald's. At the edge of town is the biggest parking lot I've ever seen; it's free, although the bus to the shrine costs a euro.

Padre Pio's image is everywhere. After dining and drinking in restaurants and wine bars, and purchasing some very cool souvenirs, I headed for nearby Monte Sant'Angelo, a far older town with some serious history, and a shrine to Saint Michele, with none of the intense tourist hype

TAVERNA LI JALANTUUMENE

Piazza de Galganis (Largo le Monache), 5

71013 Monte Sant'Angelo (FG)

Tel/Fax: +39-0884-565-484

Cell: +39-348-797-6321

info@li-jalantuumene.it

www.li-jalantuumene.it

Closed Tuesdays, October–March; closed January 8–28.

All credit cards accepted.

of San Giovanni. My friend Giulio Iannini told me about a promising restaurant with the seemingly unpronounceable name of Taverna Li Jalantuumene. When I made my reservation, chef/owner Gegé asked if I was coming on a pilgrimage (lots of people flood through town for a few hours to visit the mystical shrine), and when I informed him that I was on a gastronomic mission, he was thrilled. He couldn't stop talking about the Gargano and its unique foods: the Podolica cows (a local breed) grazing wild, the cheese made from their milk, and the lamb and pecorino cheese also from local breeds. Gegé took me to buy bread, huge eleven-pound rounds baked in a wood-burning oven, the last in the village that hadn't converted to gas or electricity. I had a new best friend.

I fell in love with Monte Sant'Angelo, the Gargano, and Taverna Li Jalantuumene, located next to a well in a charming sixteenth-century piazza. The restaurant is a three-story operation, so Gegé's wife, Ninni, races up the steep staircase that connects the two dining rooms. Food comes from the kitchen in a dumbwaiter. The menu focuses on local and seasonal products and may begin with simply sautéed ricotta flanked by a fig "must" (a local tradition of concentrated fig juice) or *salumi*. Homemade pasta—short cavatelli, orecchiette, or strands of troccoli—is sauced with something local, possibly winter squash and almonds or chickpeas and rucola (arugula). Meat like lamb, kid, or sausage is perfect with Gegé's selection of important red wines. Save room for aged cheese made from the milk of those Podolica cows. Taste the *ostie ripiene*—homemade oval wafers sandwiching a filling of whole almonds, honey, lemon, and cinnamon—and purchase a package to take home. Wine lovers should ask Gegé to visit the cellar under the well, which is stocked with an impressive selection of wines from Puglia and beyond.

BREAD MEATBALLS (WITHOUT MEAT)

SERVES 4 TO 6

4 ounces pecorino cheese, grated

4 ounces crustless rustic bread, preferably water based and made
with semolina flour, cut into cubes

4 eggs

3 garlic cloves

2 tablespoons fresh flat-leaf parsley

Freshly ground black pepper

Sea salt

1 cup plus 1 teaspoon extra virgin olive oil

2 cups canned tomatoes, puréed or diced

1 tablespoon minced fresh basil

Combine the pecorino, bread cubes, eggs, 2 of the garlic cloves, parsley, pepper, and 1 teaspoon salt in a food processor. Pulse, don't purée, until well mixed. Let mixture rest for 10 minutes so the bread absorbs the liquid. (This can be done in advance.)

Heat 1 cup of the extra virgin in a 6-inch saucepan until very hot but not smoking.

Roll rounded tablespoonfuls of the bread mixture into balls and slightly flatten them, or make quenelle-like ovals with two spoons. Fry two or three balls at a time in the olive oil until lightly browned, then drain on paper towels.

In a 10-inch skillet, sauté the remaining garlic in the 1 teaspoon oil. Add the tomatoes and bring to a simmer. Season with salt and pepper.

Add the drained balls to the sauce. Cook over low heat for 10 to 15 minutes, so that they absorb some of the tomato sauce. Garnish with basil and serve immediately.

Angelo Di Biccheri and Rocchina Lecce

PANE E SALUTE

Via Caracciolo, 13

71100 Orsara di Puglia (FO)

Tel: +39-0881-709-253

or +39-0881-755-203

www.paneesalute.it

Call to check opening times.

I WAS ON A VOYAGE of discovery with my sister Suzanne on my way home from San Giovanni Rotondo, in the northern Gargano area of Puglia. We had dinner and spent the night near the village of Orsara di Puglia. But before we left town the next morning, I had to check out a place I'd heard about called Pane e Salute, a bakery-cum-private club (so designated as to avoid Italy's overly stringent sanitary laws that govern all food producers) that once or twice a week served food baked in their ancient oven. Orsara di Puglia is a tiny village so the bakery wasn't hard to find, but it wasn't open. However, a neighbor found someone with a key and opened the dimly lit, cavelike bakery, its walls blackened by soot. Some locals stopped in and explained that the oven, from 1526, was straw burning; someone else wrapped up a few 3-kilo round loaves for us to take home.

When we got home I discovered that it was the best bread I'd ever eaten, so I organized a pilgrimage back to the village specifically to see how it was made, taking Jenn, my assistant, and her brother Josh, a chef, and others. We watched the whole process. Rocchina Lecce punched the dough by hand, followed by an overnight rise. The next morning she divided the dough into woven or plastic rising baskets; a man everyone called *uomo nero* built the fire, arranged dough mounds on a wooden baker's peel with a ten-foot handle, and inserted them into the oven. A heavy door was pushed into place to close the oven and the room filled with smoke. The bread baked for more than an hour. All this activity was followed by lunch next door—the tables had mysteriously filled with diners, including the mayor of Orsara. A progression of dishes began to appear, many featuring Orsara bread that was fried or toasted, or small loaves hollowed out and filled with vegetable soup. Lamb and potatoes were baked in the oven after the bread was removed, followed by cookies, cake, and jam tart for dessert. I've been back to the village many times and it's always a thrill.

I've become addicted to Pane e Salute's bread, which Angelo sends from Puglia wrapped in butcher paper. I use every crumb. When it is stale and completely dried out, I pound it into fantastic bread crumbs; semi-stale, in a state that can still be sliced but is too tough to eat, it's great for pancotto (page 180) or even better, a *Frittata di Pane,* which my son calls Orsara Toast—better than French toast, he claims, since he prefers the savory sauce of tomatoes to maple syrup any day. Try to find a rustic bread that's not fat-enriched and is made with all-natural yeast, *levain,* for Orsara-like results.

ORSARA TOAST

MAIN COURSE

SERVES 3 OR 4

6 eggs
5 tablespoons extra virgin olive oil
Sea salt and freshly ground black pepper
3 cups stale bread cubes (1-inch cubes)
1 cup chopped seeded tomato
1 tablespoon chopped fresh basil

Put the eggs, 1 tablespoon extra virgin, and ¼ cup water in a large bowl. Season with salt and pepper and whisk to combine. Add the bread, stir to coat all pieces, and soak, stirring every 5 minutes, for at least 15 minutes or until the bread has soaked up almost all the eggs. (Softer bread will take less time.)

(recipe continues)

Combine the tomatoes, basil, and 1 tablespoon extra virgin in a small bowl and season with salt and pepper.

Heat 2 tablespoons extra virgin in a large nonstick skillet. Add the egg-soaked bread, pressing it down into an even layer. Sauté over low heat until the frittata is solid enough to turn and golden brown underneath. Slip the frittata onto a plate, heat the remaining tablespoon extra virgin in the skillet and turn the frittata over into the skillet to cook the second side. When it is browned on the second side, slide the frittata onto a cutting board, slice into wedges, and top with some of the raw tomato sauce.

Gilberto Arru

GILBERTO ARRU, journalist for numerous publications, knows more about Sardinian food and wine than anyone else I know. He is the author of Italian guidebooks like *Il Bel Mangiare e il Buon Bere in Sardegna* and is a powerful resource for anyone touring the island. He directed me to the village of Paulilatino, where I visited the home of a woman who made ornamental breads. I watched her form flowers, leaves, and intricate decorations with sculpting tools to adorn loaves that had been made for festivities like weddings and communions. Gilberto also sent me to Oliena to see bakers making *pane carasau* or *pane carasatu* (which Gilberto told me is incorrectly but frequently called *carta da musica*), the traditional Sardinian flatbread. There I watched a woman roll out paper-thin rounds of dough with a long, narrow rolling pin; her daughter then slipped stacks of two rounds onto the floor of a wood-burning oven where they puffed up like balloons after baking for a few minutes. They were removed from the oven, separated, and then baked

IL FORNO DI MASTINI

Via Galiani, 80
08025 Oliena (NU)
Tel: +39-078-428-6091

PANIFICIO GIULIO BULLONI

Via Minerva, 2
08020 Bitti (NU)
Tel: +39-078-441-5182
panificio.bulloni@tin.it

again until lightly colored and blistered. The cooled rounds were stacked and wrapped, to be sold on the island or for export to the continent, which is how Sardinians refer to Italy.

Gilberto invited me for lunch, and I brought *pane carasau*. He warmed some up, drizzled it with extra virgin, and sprinkled it with sea salt, then we feasted on what's called *pane guttiau*. Then Gilberto made *pane frattau*, a quickly prepared one-dish meal traditionally eaten by shepherds that's made of simple, basic ingredients. He dipped pieces of flatbread into boiling water, layered them on plates with warm tomato sauce and grated pecorino, then topped it all with poached eggs, more sauce, and cheese. It's become a favorite in my kitchen, a perfect brunch or lunch dish. Look for commercial producer Giulio Bulloni's *pane carasau*—e-mail them if you can't find it, or if you're in the Sardinian province of Nuoro, visit the artisanal bakery Il Forno di Mastini in Oliena.

SARDINIAN FLATBREAD WITH TOMATO AND EGGS

MAIN COURSE

SERVES 4

2 garlic cloves, chopped

2 tablespoons extra virgin olive oil

2½ cups tomato pulp (peeled and seeded fresh tomatoes)

Sea salt and freshly ground black pepper

2 rounds *pane carasau*

1 cup grated pecorino sardo cheese (Sardinian sheep's milk cheese)

4–8 eggs

Put the garlic in a medium skillet, drizzle with the extra virgin, and sauté over medium heat until it barely begins to color. Add the tomato pulp, season with salt and pepper, and cook for 5 minutes. Keep warm.

(recipe continues)

Bring about 6 cups of water to a simmer in a skillet and add 1 to 2 tablespoons sea salt.

Break the *pane carasau* into 4- to 6-inch pieces. Neatness doesn't count. Spread ½ cup warm tomato sauce on a serving dish (or a few spoonfuls on individual serving dishes). Top with 4 tablespoons grated cheese (or a sprinkle of cheese on individual plates). Using tongs, dip a few pieces of *pane carasau* into the hot water, then layer them to completely cover the grated cheese. Top with ½ cup tomato sauce and 4 tablespoons grated cheese (less on individual plates). Dip more *pane carasau* into the water, put it on top of the previous layer, and top with ½ cup tomato sauce and 4 tablespoons cheese (less for individual plates).

Poach the eggs, one or two per person, in the hot water. The yolks should be loose.

With a slotted spoon, put the poached eggs on top of the layered *pane carasau*. Top the eggs with the remaining tomato sauce, sprinkle with remaining cheese, and serve.

Giacomo, Adele, and Tonino D'Ali

M Y FRIEND Anna Tasca Lanza and I have long been on a quest for the best Sicilian products, a journey that brought us to Giacomo D'Ali, who owns the Infersa saltpans south of Trapani. Flocks of flamingos feed in the shallow waters of the Sicilian seacoast, alongside elongated pyramids of salt neatly covered with terra-cotta roof tiles by the side of the road. Giacomo took us to his restored windmill (across from the island of Mozia, an eighth-century B.C. Phoenician stronghold) that was once used to pump water from one pan to another and to grind salt. He showed us the factory where salt is packaged and processed, and I had lots of questions. Why was his salt pure white, unlike the finest

French salt? "Because French salt is dirty," he responded. Why was his salt dry? "Because in Sicily, salt is dried by the sun and wind, and wet salt would ruin the cardboard box" answered Giacomo. I was hooked by the flavor of *sale integrale,* or unwashed sea salt—just like a mouthful of the Mediterranean—and its attractive packaging, with MOTHIA written in large letters and a picture of the sea, a windmill, and a flamingo. I brought lots of salt home, and now many of my friends in Florence are converts.

On a subsequent visit I met Giacomo's son Tonino and his wife Adele, who showed me the inn they had recently restored, La Finestra sul Sale (A Window on Salt), across from the saltpans and windmill. Adele introduced me to her most special salt, *soffi di sale*—fine crystals blown by the wind to the edges of the saltpans—and gave me a recipe for Fish Baked Under Sicilian Sea Salt. Both the wind-blown salt and her recipe provide culinary thrills. Beginners will probably want to add egg whites to the salt so that, once baked, the salt crust comes off more easily.

SOSALT SPA

Zona Ronciglio
91100 Trapani
Tel: +39-0923-540-344
Fax: +39-0923-202-81
info@sosalt.com
www.sosalt.it

LA FINESTRA SUL SALE

Bed & Breakfast
Contrada Ettore Infersa, 158
91025 Marsala (TP)
Tel: +39-0923-966-936
Fax: +39-0923-733-142
estrasulsale@sicilia.indettaglio.it

FISH BAKED UNDER SICILIAN SEA SALT

SERVES 4

½ teaspoon fennel pollen or seeds

1 sprig fresh rosemary

3–3½-pound freshest possible whole fish,
   such as sea bass or snapper

5 pounds Sicilian sea salt

2 egg whites (optional)

3 tablespoons extra virgin olive oil

1 lemon (optional)

Preheat the oven to 400°F.

Put the fennel pollen or seeds and rosemary sprig in the cavity of the fish. Mix the sea salt with 1 cup water, and add more, a few teaspoons at a time, until the mixture is like wet sand—perfect for building sand castles. For an easier-to-remove salt crust, add lightly beaten egg whites to the salt before adding additional water. (This isn't the Sicilian way, unnecessary with Sicilian sea salt, but it's an option.) Place a ¾-inch layer of wet salt slightly larger than the fish on a nonstick baking pan or pan lined with a nonstick mat. Put the fish on the salt and mold the rest of the salt to encase the fish completely.

Bake the fish for 20 to 25 minutes or until the salt has completely hardened and formed a crust. Remove from the oven. For tableside presentation, put the fish on a large platter. Crack the salt crust with a mallet (or any suitable instrument) and remove the pieces from the fish. Remove the skin and divide the fish into fillets. Remove the cheeks. Place the boned fish and cheeks on a platter or individual serving dishes and drizzle with extra virgin and a squeeze of lemon juice, if desired.

* * *

Antonietta Rotonda

ANTONIETTA ROTONDA runs a wonderful *agriturismo* farm inn, Terra di Conca, not too far from her husband Berardino Lombardo's restaurant inn (page 179), where we met for the first time. They bought the farm in a state of total abandon, the house an uninhabitable, roofless ruin, and have lovingly resurrected it, now dedicated to cultivating the local foods. Berardino and Antonietta began with black pigs—a native breed—and poultry such as guinea hens, chickens, and capons to supply his restaurant. Later he grafted the heirloom fruit trees (over twelve kinds of local apples!) growing wild on the property and planted saved seeds for local tomatoes, greens, eggplants, and squash. Antonietta guided the restoration of the house. It's appropriately rustic, with a large open fireplace surrounded by sofas in the living room and a table nearby where guests both breakfast and dine in the evening. Antonietta is one of Italy's most important collectors of antique lace from the sixteenth to twentieth centuries, and some of her pieces are displayed in the living room. Lace-trimmed or embroidered linens in the bedrooms are a joy to sleep on. Ask to see her extensive collection of handkerchiefs, from a time when the handkerchief was a most important fashion accessory.

TERRA DI CONCA
Via Piantoli
Conca della Campania (CE)
Tel: +39-339-592-8649
No credit cards.

Antonietta does all the cooking at the farm, utilizing produce straight from her organic garden. I hung out in her kitchen as she prepared dinner, which included two vegetable dishes; both were so terrific and easy that I couldn't decide which recipe to ask for, so I got them both. Poor Little Eggplants is a family tradition from Antonietta's perennially fund-less aunt, who scavenged eggplant, foraged herbs, and produced a tasty dish with a few inexpensive ingredients. Everyone's favorite Antonietta's Baked Cherry Tomatoes are also always on the menu at Berardino's restaurant, La Caveja. Visit Terra di Conca to taste them at their very best.

POOR LITTLE EGGPLANTS

SERVES 4 TO 6

6 small, long eggplants (sometimes called Japanese eggplants,
    4–6 inches long, no more than 2 inches in diameter)
6 garlic cloves, sliced
3 tablespoons fresh or dried (but not old) oregano
2 teaspoons fine sea salt
¼ cup extra virgin olive oil
3 tablespoons red wine vinegar

Preheat the oven to 500°F.

Slice the eggplants lengthwise and score the cut surface with a knife, making parallel diagonal incisions, then making parallel diagonal incisions in the other direction.

Scatter the sliced garlic, oregano, and salt in a 10½ by 15-inch baking pan. Pour the extra virgin and vinegar into the pan. Place the eggplants cut side down in one layer in the baking pan.

Bake for 25 to 30 minutes or until the eggplants are tender.

BAKED CHERRY TOMATOES

SERVES 4 TO 6

36 cherry tomatoes
¼ cup bread crumbs
2 tablespoons fresh or dried (but not old) oregano
3 garlic cloves
Fine sea salt and pepper
2 tablespoons extra virgin olive oil

Preheat the oven to 400°F.

Halve the cherry tomatoes. Chop the bread crumbs, oregano, and garlic together until the garlic is minced. Season with salt and pepper.

Drizzle 1 teaspoon extra virgin on the bottom of a 10 by 12-inch baking pan (glass, nonstick, or lined with foil). Place half of the cherry tomato halves, split side up, in a layer in the pan. Sprinkle the tomatoes with the crumb and herb mixture. Top with the remaining tomato halves, rounded side up, to reform the tomatoes. Drizzle the remaining extra virgin on top of the tomatoes.

Bake for 25 to 30 minutes or until lightly browned.

Gennaro and Salvatore Canfora; Patrizia Arcini

I WAS WANDERING through Naples when I happened upon an interesting grocery with a large display of Setaro's fine pasta in the window. Since a visit to Torre Annunziata to visit Setaro was already on the agenda for that afternoon, I felt compelled to enter the shop. Owner Gennaro Canfora and his wife, Patrizia Arcini, were behind the counter, and when I complimented Gennaro on his pasta selection, he launched into a discussion of quality local ingredients. To demonstrate, he insisted that I taste the provolone he had aged for over two years, and I became an instant convert.

In addition to the pasta, pizza with escarole, a display counter of fine cheese and *salumi,* a refrigerator filled with interesting and well-priced wines, and Gennaro's enthusiasm made this shop a fantastic find. Even better, the meals cooked by Gennaro's son Salvatore were served at tables outside the shop beneath a wine-colored awning that read "Very Naples Cooking." I promised to come back for dinner, not only because I was tempted by the cheese and *salumi* but also because Gennaro goes to the fish market in the afternoon when the boats come in and buys the freshest fish he can find. I returned with Neapolitan friends, and after choosing our regional wines, we dug into two kinds of eggplant, braised escarole, marinated olives, and *salumi* to start. Next came pasta with tiny clams. The star of the meal, though, was red mullet —super-fresh and deep-fried in a "double shirt" of batter that serves as insulation and is removed to reveal moist, delicate fish that needs no condiment.

Gennaro has purchased a neighboring shop and is now serving meals inside as well as under the awning, and though he's been discovered by guidebooks, it's still a bargain. Since few of us can get fish fresh enough to make Salvatore's "double shirt" mullet, I asked for his recipe for Braised Escarole, my favorite vegetable preparation and always on his menu.

OSTERIA DEGLI ANTICHI SAPORI

Via Santa Lucia, 18
80100 Napoli
Tel: +39-081-245-1183
Closed Sundays.

SIDE DISH

BRAISED ESCAROLE

SERVES 4 TO 6

4–6 medium heads of escarole, around 1½ pounds

2 tablespoons capers packed in salt

Coarse and fine sea salt

¼ cup extra virgin olive oil

2 garlic cloves, peeled

2–3 anchovy fillets

¼ cup pitted green olives, coarsely chopped (Salvatore prefers Gaeta olives)

1 chili pepper (optional)

Cut a slice off the root ends of the escarole heads and remove any bruised outer leaves. Spread the leaves to separate the heads and rinse the escarole in a sinkful of warm water. Don't worry if some of the leaves detach. Cut each head in half.

Soak the capers in 1 cup water for 10 minutes to remove the excess salt. Rinse, squeeze out the excess water, and set aside.

Bring 5 quarts of water to a rolling boil. Add 3 tablespoons coarse salt and the escarole heads, and cook for 6 to 8 minutes, until tender when poked with a knife. Reserve a cup of the vegetable-cooking water and refresh the escarole in a sinkful of cold water. Remove to a strainer and then press to remove excess water.

Heat the extra virgin in a large skillet. Add the garlic cloves and sauté until they barely begin to color. Add the anchovies and mash them with a wooden spoon to dissolve, then add the olives, capers, and escarole (and optional chili pepper), and sauté over low heat for 10 to 15 minutes. Add some of the vegetable-cooking water if mixture dries out. Taste for salt (anchovies and capers will contribute salt to the dish so it's added at the end), and serve hot or at room temperature.

Tonino and Mary Simeti

I READ MARY SIMETI'S wonderful book *On Persephone's Island* before a month-long trip to Sicily and when I arrived in Palermo, I called Mary to invite her to lunch. We had a lot in common: expatriated Americans integrated into an Italian way of life, with Italian husbands, kids in the Italian school system, both of us writing for U.S. publications. Mary invited me to Bosco, her home in the countryside outside Palermo, and I met her husband Tonino, the *professore* (an important title in Italy), who taught agricultural studies at the university; he has become a terrific source of information about Sicilian crops like citrus, almonds, and pistachio nuts.

Mary and I went on holiday together to the island of Pantelleria, organized by our mutual friend Anna Tasca Lanza (I introduced them, as both are interested in Sicilian traditions), and were joined by our husbands, Anna's sisters and their partners, and a few friends. We stayed in rustic cottages, swam, shopped, and cooked together; ate raw sea urchins fished by a fellow guest; and dined outside on the terrace, overlooking the sea. The main topic of conversation was food. Mary and Tonino reminisced about the artichokes, flavored with mint and garlic and roasted in embers, that they made for friends and family on *Pasquetta,* or "Little Easter" (the Monday after Easter Sunday). The outer leaves get completely charred and are peeled away. It sounded too simple to resist, too delicious to reserve for an annual cookout. Fortunately, since I live in the city, I discovered I can roast the artichokes in the oven with nearly as delectable results.

MARY SIMETI WROTE:

On Persephone's Island
Pomp and Sustenance:
*   Twenty-Five Centuries of*
*   Sicilian Food*
Bitter Almonds: Recollections
*   and Recipes from a Sicilian*
*   Girlhood*

SIDE DISH

"LITTLE EASTER" ROASTED ARTICHOKES

SERVES 6

6 garlic cloves
⅓–½ cup tightly packed fresh mint leaves
1 teaspoon fine sea salt
Freshly ground black pepper or red pepper flakes
6 medium to large artichokes, as fresh as possible (if only small
    artichokes are available, use twice as many)
¼ cup extra virgin olive oil

Build a wood or charcoal fire, or preheat the oven to 475°F.

Mince the garlic and mint and combine with the salt and pepper or red pepper flakes.

Slice the stem ends of the artichokes to level them so that they can stand in a baking pan. Cut the top third off the artichokes but don't bother to trim off the tough leaves. Pry open the leaves of the artichokes (or press them on a clean surface, stem side up) to make room for the mint-garlic mixture. Push some of the herb-garlic mixture between the leaves of the artichokes. Neatness doesn't count.

Drizzle the extra virgin into the center of the artichokes and roast them directly on ember-coated coals, turning frequently, to be truly authentic. Or stand the artichokes on a foil-lined baking pan, drizzle the centers with extra virgin, and roast for 40 to 45 minutes, or until the outer leaves are dark and dried.

Eat the tender parts of the leaves, remove the choke, and then eat the heart—with your fingers when cool enough to handle. (Don't wear silk—this is an oily, messy, but delicious way to eat artichokes.)

Lucia and Rino Botte, Leonardo Pietrafesa, and Carla Podolica-Pucillo

TWO OF the exceptional people I met while I was researching the first edition of *Eating in Italy* were Lucia and Rino Botte. They had relocated to the north from Basilicata, and the restaurant they established in Cremona, Cerasuole, was highly rated in guidebooks. Like most Italians, though, they longed for home and eventually transferred to Barile, where Lucia's family owned a winery. When they opened an elegant inn, I planned a visit. Just before my trip, I had lunch in Rome with Tonino and Caterina Palmieri (page 232), and met the Palmieris' interior designer, to whom I was introduced as an important American journalist.

LOCANDA DEL PALAZZO

Piazza Largo Caracciolo, 7
85022 Barile (PZ)
Tel/Fax: +39-0972-771-051
locandadelpalazzo@libero.it
www.locandadelpalazzo.com
Closed Sunday dinner and
Mondays; closed 15 days in
February and July 15–30.
All credit cards accepted.

TENUTA LE QUERCE

Contrada le Querce
85100 Barile (PZ)
Tel: +39-0971-470-709
or +39-0972-725-102
Visits by appointment only.

"More important than Parker?" she asked. I asked how a Roman decorator knew about Parker, and she told me her husband, Leonardo, had a winery in Barile, Tenuta le Querce. Since I was leaving for Barile the next week, I added the winery to my list of destinations.

The Locanda del Palazzo—eleven elegantly appointed rooms with super bathrooms—was a perfect base for touring the area. We had a wonderful tasting at Tenuta le Querce, where the owner, Leonardo Pietrafesa, and marketing director Carla Podolica-Pucillo offered us three different versions of local red cultivar Aglianico del Vulture: Il Viola, the simplest; Rosso di Costanza and Vigna della Corona (single vineyard), both aged in barriques; and Tamurro Nero, an ancient varietal grown only by Tenuta le Querce. We invited Leonardo and Carla back to the Locanda for lunch, and were joined there by Puccio and friends from the Oasis restaurant (page 228).

The restaurant is spacious and beautifully appointed, with linens, crystal, silver, and a hilltop view of vineyards, Monte Vulture in the distance. We feasted on Lucia's inspired versions of regional dishes, like homemade hard-wheat cavatelli and roast lamb and we drank Tenuta le Querce's wines. Dessert was a wonderful walnut cake, and when I asked Lucia for the recipe, I discovered it was like no other cake recipe I've ever encountered: no flour, no fat, only three ingredients, and a pinch of salt. Lucia beats half the egg whites and sugar into a meringue and heats the other half to make a melted marshmallow-like batter; walnuts are then folded in. Superior walnuts are imperative for this recipe, so substitute pecans, hazelnuts, or almonds if their quality is better.

LUCIA'S WALNUT CAKE

SERVES 6 TO 8

Oil for greasing the pan

6 egg whites, at room temperature

⅓ cup plus 2 tablespoons sugar

Pinch of sea salt

2 cups coarsely chopped walnuts

Preheat the oven to 350°F. Do not use a convection oven. Line the bottom of an 8-inch springform pan with parchment paper. Lightly oil the paper and sides of the pan.

Combine 3 egg whites and ⅓ cup sugar in a heavy saucepan and stir over low heat with a wooden spoon until the mixture looks like white slush—like melted marshmallows. This may take 10 minutes or more.

Beat the remaining 3 egg whites with a pinch of salt in a large bowl until stiff.

Combine the cooked egg whites with the chopped walnuts. Stir some of the beaten egg whites into the walnut mixture and fold the remaining whites in carefully. Transfer the batter to the pan, sprinkle the top with the remaining 2 tablespoons sugar, and bake for 55 to 60 minutes, until a toothpick comes out dry.

* * *

Fischetti Family

OASIS-SAPORI ANTICHI

Via Provinciale Vallesaccarda
83050 Vallesaccarda (AV)
Tel: +39-0827-970-21
Fax: +39-0827-975-41
info@oasis-saporiantichi.it
www.oasis-saporiantichi.it
Closed Thursdays and Sunday
evenings; closed July 1–15.
Reservations required.
All credit cards accepted.

THE FISCHETTI FAMILY'S aptly named restaurant, Oasis, is located in the village of Vallesaccarda, five kilometers from the barren highway that connects Naples and Bari. Everyone in this gigantic family—Papa Generoso and Mamma Giuseppina daughters Maria Luisa and Lina; son Carmine and his wife, Maria Grazia; son Puccio and his wife, Raffaela; son Nicolo and his fiancée, Silvana; and cousins Domenico, Marco, Anna, Giusi, and Serena—plays a role in the restaurant. Carmine has taken me to visit nearby wineries, Puccio to local artisans of their area, known as the Baronie. Giuseppina, Lina, Maria Lusia, and Maria Grazia have taken me into their kitchens and taught me how to hand-form pasta. What's not to love?

Offering a careful reworking of tradition, Oasis features food that is lightened up but not fancified. It began life as a bar, run by Generoso and Giuseppina, that served hot soups to the workers building the highway nearby. When the restaurant caught on, Fischetti sons and daughters returned from restaurant jobs elsewhere, pitched in, expanded the menu (keeping the hearty soups), and added a serious wine list. Homemade pasta, local lamb and pork, and produce straight from the farm are all prepared with elegance. The menu is lengthy, though reasonably priced tasting menus of varying lengths simplify things. Begin with an antipasto medley of local *salumi,* cupcake-size baskets of just-made ricotta, escarole and bean crostini, or potato, onion, and sweet pepper salad. First-course bean soups or handmade organic hard-wheat pasta sauced with meat or vegetables are followed by local lamb, kid, rabbit, and spicy pork sausage. Desserts like ricotta and sour cherry tart or torrone semifreddo with chocolate sauce tempt, but I never fail to sample the chocolate espresso dessert with its soft hot center, baked in an espresso cup—a cross between a soufflé and a hot chocolate pudding, with a serious, grown-up hit of coffee.

CHOCOLATE-ESPRESSO SOUFFLÉ

DESSERT

SERVES 6 TO 8

Oil for greasing the cups
3 tablespoons butter
3½ ounces finest quality (70 percent) bittersweet chocolate
4 teaspoons brewed espresso coffee
2 tablespoons soft wheat flour (Italians "00" or White Lily flour)
3½ tablespoons ground coffee for espresso
2 eggs, separated
1½ tablespoons sugar
Pinch of sea salt

Preheat the oven to 400°F. Lightly oil six to eight espresso cups.

Combine the butter, chocolate, and brewed espresso coffee in a small bowl and melt over hot water or in a microwave. Stir to combine, then cool.

Mix the flour and ground espresso coffee. Beat the egg yolks with the sugar until pale yellow. In a separate bowl, beat the egg whites with a pinch of salt until stiff. Add the cooled chocolate mixture to the beaten yolks and combine. Fold in the flour and espresso mixture, then fold in the beaten whites. Divide the mixture among the prepared espresso cups. (This can be done up to 6 hours in advance and refrigerated. Let them come to room temperature before baking.) Bake for 5 to 6 minutes. Serve hot or warm.

Franco, Antonio, and Carla Sersale

LE SIRENUSE

Via C. Colombo, 30

84017 Positano (SA)

Tel: +39-089-875-066

Fax: +39-089-811-798

info@sirenuse.it

www.lesirenuse.com

EAU D'ITALIE S.R.L.

Corso del Popolo, 71

00046 Grottaferrata (RM)

Tel/Fax: +39-06-687-2340

info@eauditalie.it

www.eauditalie.it

Visits by appointment only.

THE SERSALE FAMILY owns Le Sirenuse, one of Italy's greatest hotels, in Positano, on the Amalfi Coast. I first met Franco in the early 1980s, when I stayed at the hotel to write about Le Sirenuse's pasta party (twenty different kinds of pasta, all perfectly cooked, served at a buffet, with an equally ample dessert selection) for an Italian magazine. It was easy to fall in love with the hotel, which boasts terraced rooms with a view of the sea, exceptional service, and the personal attention of Franco Sersale and his siblings. The hotel began as a rustic family summer home; originally the Sersales lived in Naples for most of the year, though after World War II they took up residence in Positano. Plenty of friends came to stay with them, and they eventually decided to turn their villa into a small luxury hotel. Over the years the Sersale family has purchased neighboring buildings, expanding the hotel into a labyrinth of rooms with hand-painted ceramic tile floors, comfortable sitting rooms, eighteenth-century country home decor, and potted orchids, vines, and flowers everywhere.

Franco's son Antonio manages the hotel, and Antonio's wife Carla is in charge of the Emporio boutique. They're both responsible for many of the innovations at the hotel. Le Sirenuse has its own line of amenities, called Eau d'Italie, that are simply the best of any hotel I've ever stayed at. Summer guests get a transparent pouch of sun-protection products. The restaurant, La Sponda, is illuminated by candlelight in the evening, and is one of the most romantic dining settings I've ever encountered. The Champagne and Oyster Bars serve Mediterranean appetizers, oysters, raw fish and seafood, sparkling wines and cocktails on two upper terraces, perfect for sunset viewing or stargazing. The Swimming Pool Caffè offers salads, sandwiches, and snacks for those who don't want to dress for lunch or miss a moment of sun. Le Sirenuse has kept pace with the times, with a Gae Aulenti-designed gym and spa. And to complete the experience, shop the Emporio boutiques, where Carla personally selects all the items. Look for glassware (Venetian glass designed for the hotel) and dinnerware (designed by Carla's sister, Costanza Paravicini) in the hotel, stylish clothing and accessories across the street.

Regional research is my excuse for a visit to Le Sirenuse—to check out new restaurants with Antonio, Carla, and Franco. When I can't visit, I go to the website to take in the webcam view of the sea from Le Sirenuse's terrace, and I think about the Pineapple Carpaccio with Pineapple Sorbetto served at La Sponda. It's one of the most refreshing desserts I've ever tasted. Those with ice cream machines should slice the pineapple first, then churn the sorbetto. Readers who are really in a hurry can simply slice and sugar fresh pineapple, then top it with purchased pineapple sorbet.

PINEAPPLE CARPACCIO WITH PINEAPPLE SORBETTO

DESSERT

SERVES 4

1½ cups pineapple cubes
½ cup granulated sugar, or more if pineapple purée is tart
Pinch of sea salt
8 ounces fresh pineapple, cored and trimmed
3 tablespoons confectioners' sugar
8 fresh mint leaves

Place the pineapple cubes in a food processor and process until puréed. Measure out 1½ cups and set aside. Bring 1½ cups water and the granulated sugar to a boil in a small pot and boil for 3 minutes. Cool the syrup and combine with the pineapple purée and the salt. Freeze the mixture in an ice cream machine according to manufacturer's directions.

(recipe continues)

While the sorbetto is churning, slice the remaining pineapple into the thinnest possible rounds. Divide the slices onto four plates and dust the confectioners' sugar over the slices.

When the sorbetto is done, place 2 scoops on each plate of pineapple slices. Garnish each with 2 mint leaves and serve immediately. (Sorbetto will hold in the freezer for 45 minutes, but should ideally be eaten fresh. If left too long in the freezer it will turn into a rock and need to be melted and rechurned.)

Tonino and Caterina Palmieri

TONINO PALMIERI is the best, and most handsome, buffalo mozzarella producer in Italy. The road south of Battipaglia is lined with big signs advertising buffalo mozzarella stores, but Tonino's farm, Tenuta Vannulo, isn't easy to spot. The sign is tiny, and a narrow driveway leads to the retail shop.

Tonino took me to look around his farm. Water buffalo usually hang out in a pool of mud to keep their skin damp and cool, but Tonino thinks it's not hygienic and will eventually be banned by the European Union sanitation laws. So his buffalo are misted with a spray of water when it's hot and they sleep on rubber mattresses, not on the muddy ground. Cleaner buffalo don't have to be aggressively washed before milking, and since they are more relaxed when they approach the milking machines, they actually give more milk. The buffalo are medicated, when necessary, with homeopathic medicine.

Unlike the other producers, Tonino Palmieri grows organic feed for his buffalo, who in turn produce organic milk. All this innovative obsession yields better milk, which is transformed, unpasteurized, into mozzarella, ricotta, yogurt, and puddings—all sold at the shop. (They are never shipped because shipping requires refrigeration, and mozzarella should be stored at room temperature, never lower, or the texture is drastically altered.) Restaurateurs, local gastronomes, and manic mozzarella freaks make the pilgrimage to the shop at Tenuta Vannulo, which is usually sold out by noon. After scoring some mozzarella, most clients head for the bar-yogurteria for an espresso, perhaps "stained" with steamed buffalo milk. Buffalo yogurt, either plain or flavored with fruit (organic, of course) and topped with Vannulo's honey, is also available to eat at the counter or tables or sold to go, in adorable little screw-top glass jars. There's also unbelievably rich buffalo milk gelato in seasonal fruit flavors, chocolate, or coffee. The newest product is buffalo milk puddings— white, milk, bittersweet chocolate, and coffee—sold in the same jars as the yogurt.

On my second visit, Tonino invited me home for lunch with his wife, Caterina, who is beautiful, hospitable, and lactose intolerant. Our lunch (but not hers) began with the morning's mozzarella, oozing with whey— far more delicate than mozzarella that's a day or two old. We then had pasta, a buffalo meat course, and many desserts. My favorite was buffalo ricotta, served in the center of a lazy-susan containing chocolate, honey, homemade kumquat preserves, sugar, cinnamon, and ground espresso coffee—a kind of do-it-yourself ricotta sundae. Even with a lesser ricotta than Tenuta Vannulo's it's still a fantastic dessert.

TENUTA VANNULO

Via G. Galilei (Contrada Vannulo)
84040 Capaccio Scalo (SA)
Tel: +39-0828-724-765
Fax: +39-0828-725-245
www.vannulo.it
Open to the public; call or fax for an appointment.

RICOTTA WITH CONDIMENTS

SERVES 6 TO 8

1½ pounds fresh whole-milk ricotta
Any or all of the following condiments:
    Chopped bittersweet chocolate
    Finely ground coffee
    Cinnamon
    Honey
    Orange marmalade
    Fresh berries
    Sugar

Drain the ricotta in a sieve if it appears watery. Line a 4-cup woven basket (for a rustic look), bowl, or mold with plastic wrap. Pack the ricotta into the basket or mold, pressing with a spatula. Cover with the edges of the plastic wrap and refrigerate until serving.

Place the condiments in small bowls. Unmold the ricotta, removing the plastic wrap, onto an attractive plate. Serve with condiments.

Vito, Antonietta, Viviana, and Dorianna Santoro

How did I ever live without Vito Santoro? We met when I was looking for a driver for a trip through Campania with a group of food-loving friends. I hired an eighteen-seater bus, Vito showed up on time with a fifty-two-seater, and explained that "the other bus had mechanical problems." He declared himself an *artista* (artist), not *autista* (driver), and was always ready to solve any problem, to navigate any road or menu—all serious tasks on my itineraries. We visited wineries and restaurants, food artisans and museums. When we neared his village of Scampitella, he invited all twelve of us gastronauts to his home for a glass of wine and cookies prepared by his wife, Antonietta. For the final dinner of our trip, Vito hired a duo of accordion players to serenade us. When the trip was over, I had a new friend.

SANTORO AUTOTRASPORTI/ SANTORO VIAGGI

Via Piano di Contra, 20
83050 Scampitella (AV)
Tel/Fax: +39-0827-934-03
Cell: +39-329-618-8787
autotrasporti@vitosantoro.com
www.vitosantoro.com

Since that fateful first trip, Vito has accompanied me all over Italy, from the Alps to Sicily, to the Salone del Gusto in Torino and VinItaly in Verona, arranging transport of purchases and people, always with a smile. In turn, I shop for cool American sportswear for Vito's daughters, Viviana and Dorianna, on my visits to the states. We've had Easter lunch at Vito's with his whole family, friends with nicknames like Plix and Ross, and even the village priest, Don Erminio. My sister Suzanne's painting of Vito's *carta d'identita* inspired her to undertake all the illustrations for this book. In short, he's family.

I'm crazy about Antonietta's jam-stuffed cookies, made with homemade candied sour cherry preserves—she served them on my first visit to her kitchen.

PRESERVE-FILLED BISCOTTI

MAKES 12 TO 14 COOKIES

7 tablespoons butter, at room temperature

½ cup sugar

2 egg yolks

1 teaspoon grated lemon zest

1½ cups soft wheat flour (Italian "00" or White Lily flour)

¼ teaspoon sea salt

¼ cup sour cherry preserves

Cream the butter and sugar, then mix in the egg yolks and lemon zest until light and fluffy. Stir together the flour and salt, then blend with the creamed butter mixture. Form the dough into a ball and refrigerate for an hour or more.

Preheat the oven to 350°F.

Cut the dough into two pieces and roll each piece into a "snake" 12 to 15 inches long and 1 inch in diameter. Cut off 1-inch pieces and roll each into a ball, then press your thumb into each piece to form a little well. Put a scant ¼ teaspoon of preserves in each well (if you put too much it will ooze out when you pinch it closed), and press the dough over the preserves to completely enclose it in the dough. Place sealed side down on a baking sheet lined with parchment paper or a nonstick baking mat.

Bake for 10 to 15 minutes, until lightly browned. Transfer to a wire rack to cool.

＊　＊　＊

Agata Parisella and Romeo and Marianetta Caraccio

AGATA PARISELLA and her husband Romeo Caraccio took over her family's Roman trattoria with the dream of turning it into a serious restaurant. She had studied cooking and pastry with important Italian and French chefs and, more importantly, in her mother and grand-mother's kitchens, and wanted to lighten up Roman dishes and experi-ment with non-Roman foods and recipes. Sommelier Romeo was obsessed with service and wanted to create a serious wine list to go with his wife's cooking. They remodeled, upgraded the crystal, linen, and silver and put their daughter Marianetta in charge of the impressive cheese selection. The result was a world-class restaurant with two menus—traditional dishes improved by technique and creative seasonal dishes—both utiliz-ing the finest foods that Romeo can source.

Whenever I visit we reminisce about the restaurant's beginnings, and this dessert has been on the menu from the very start. It's a huge improvement on classic *millefoglie,* a structured puff pastry sandwich of "one thousand leaves" filled with whipped cream-custard that is always a disappointment since the pastry gets soggy. Agata's version is assembled at the last minute and has a sloppy but attractive look, the just-crumbled puff pastry scattered on a plate, topped with light custard and almonds, finished with more crumbled pastry and a dusting of confectioners' sugar. You can bake the pastry and prepare the custard up to a day in advance.

AGATA E ROMEO

Via Carlo Alberto, 45
00185 Roma
Tel: +39-06-446-6115
Fax: +39-06-446-5842
www.agataeromeo.it
ristorante@agataeromeo.it
Closed Saturdays and Sundays;
closed January 1-16 and
August 6-27. All credit cards
accepted.

AGATA E ROMEO'S MILLEFOGLIE

SERVES 6 TO 8

1 cup milk

2-inch piece vanilla bean

1 strip lemon zest (around 2 inches)

2 egg yolks

¼ cup granulated sugar

3 tablespoons flour

1 cup heavy cream

½ pound puff pastry, baked according to package directions
    and cooled

½ cup sliced almonds, toasted

Confectioners' sugar

In a small saucepan, scald the milk with the vanilla bean and lemon peel.

In a large mixing bowl, beat the egg yolks and granulated sugar until thick and pale yellow. Stir in the flour until completely blended.

Remove the lemon peel and vanilla bean from the milk and whip the hot milk into the egg mixture until smooth. Cook the mixture, stirring constantly with a whisk over low heat until it barely boils. Pour into a bowl, cover with plastic wrap, and cool completely.

Whip the cream until stiff, then fold it gently into the cooled custard. Chill if not using immediately.

To serve: Divide the puff pastry into 6 to 8 pieces, one for each serving. Coarsely crumble half a piece of puff pastry onto each of 6 to 8 plates. Top with 3 to 4 tablespoons custard. Top the custard with some toasted sliced almonds, then crumble the remaining puff pastry over all and sprinkle with confectioners' sugar. Serve immediately.

* * *

Giuseppe and Pasquale Alongi; Fatima Alves

I'M A GELATO FREAK and love the intensity of the flavors, so different (less air, less chill, less fat) from ice cream. Truly great gelato isn't easy to find, so when I tasted the Alongi brothers' gelato at a restaurant in Rome, I took a cab directly from the restaurant to San Crispino, the brothers' gelateria located in a residential neighborhood outside the historic center of Rome. Giuseppe and Pasquale were behind a stainless-steel counter, where sunken tubs of gelato were covered with stainless-steel lids—so unlike the usual displays found in most gelaterie. The brothers solemnly informed me that they kept their gelato hidden because it was stored at exactly the right temperature, without ventilation, and served only in cups; cones have artificial flavoring. There are absolutely no fake flavors or colors, preservatives, or emulsifiers in San Crispino's gelatos and sorbets, just seasonal fruit (never frozen pulp), whole fresh eggs, milk, hazelnuts from Piemonte, aged rum, the finest Marsala, Blue Mountain coffee from Jamaica, and pistachio nuts from Sicily. The house specialty, San Crispino, is rich and eggy, flavored with *corbezzolo* (strawberry tree) honey from a World Wildlife Fund preserve in Sardinia. Most gelaterie make two bases, white and custard, that are then flavored, sometimes with mixes; at San Crispino, each flavor is made from scratch, with its own calibrated formula.

Giuseppppe and Pasquale have opened a new, larger laboratory outside the center of Rome and a gelateria around the corner from the Trevi fountain that is more convenient for visitors than the original location. It's a small, narrow shop, not as flashy as the gelaterie closer to the Trevi fountain that attract hoards of tourists. Fatima Alves is behind the counter, taking orders, and the flavors are listed in English and Italian. Look for a small crowd outside the entrance, spooning up gelato and sorbetto with ecstatic expressions.

IL GELATO DI SAN CRISPINO

Via Acaia, 56
00183 Roma
Tel: +39-06-704-50412

Via della Panetteria, 42
00187 Roma
Tel: +39-06-679-3924

Via Bevagna, 90
00191 Roma
Tel: +39-06-332-1075

info@ilgelatodisancrispino.com
www.ilgelatodisancrispino.com
All are closed Tuesdays.

Here's the formula for fruit sorbetto the way it's made at San Crispino. Add more or less sugar according to an individual fruit's sweetness, degree of ripeness, and your personal taste.

For best consistency, eat it immediately after freezing in your ice cream machine, or if placed in the freezer, within 45 minutes.

DESSERT

FRUIT GELATO

SERVES 4 TO 6

½ cup sugar or more (see Note)
1¼ cups puréed fruit pulp, strained if desired
1 cup boiling water
1 tablespoon lemon juice
⅛ teaspoon sea salt

Dissolve the sugar in boiling water, mix with the remaining ingredients, and freeze in an ice-cream machine according to the manufacturer's directions, usually 20 to 25 minutes. (Nonelectric machines with an insert that goes in the freezer will take longer, up to 35 or 40 minutes.) Place the gelato in a container in the refrigerator to ripen for 30 to 45 minutes; if left too long in the freezer, it will get too hard to spoon.

NOTE: Fruits high in sugar, like grape, banana, and mango, will be fine with ½ cup sugar. Taste, and if mixture doesn't seem sweet enough, add a tablespoon of sugar at a time until the desired sweetness is achieved. Blueberries, cherries, pineapples, papaya, figs, plums, tangerines, and apricots have less sugar and will need an extra tablespoon or two of sugar, added one at a time, then tasted. Strawberry, blackberry, raspberry, peach, melon, orange, and grapefruit have lower sugar contents also, and will need 2 or 3 tablespoons extra sugar, depending on the fruit.

Silvano Paris

W HEN I MOVED to Rome in the early '70s I decided that I
wanted to learn about regional Italian cooking. I wrote a letter
to the president of the Accademia della Cucina Italiana, a culinary association, asking for suggestions, such as a restaurant where I could learn. He
recommended two restaurants, and when I presented his letter to Silvano
Paris, who owned a restaurant in Trastevere not far from my apartment,
Silvano was amused—an American woman who wanted to learn about
Italian cooking was unheard of. Eventually, though, the restaurant
adopted me. Silvano took me food shopping: to the Roman wholesale
market at dawn, and on excursions to the family farm outside the city for
wine, fruit, and cases of tomatoes in the summer. I worked in the
kitchen, taking orders from chef Mario, snapping the ends off green
beans, peeling garlic, rolling cannelloni, or cleaning a case of anchovies, a
totally new experience for me. After sharing the staff lunch, I'd observe
the lunch shift, with all its last-minute preparations, and I carefully took
notes. The menu was classic Roman—pasta dishes like carbonara and
amatriciana, saltimbocca, chicken with peppers, grilled baby lamb chops,
and fresh fish. I learned how to clean and prepare vegetables I'd never
encountered, like *puntarelle,* or Catalan chicory that must be peeled,
pared, and soaked; huge artichokes on stems with leaves, which were
trimmed to be totally edible; ripe red and yellow peppers (I knew only
green) to be roasted and peeled; bitter greens like broccoletti and rape,
and rughetta, or wild arugula. I watched Renato, a master of timing, prepare pasta and gnocchi, each order beginning with sauce in a skillet to
which drained pasta or gnocchi were added, then swirled, stirred, and
tossed with the sauce to finish the cooking and "marry" the pasta or
gnocchi to the sauce—a technique I'd never seen before. He manipulated
multiple skillets, with single, double, or larger portions of different pastas

PARIS
(under new management)
Piazza San Carlo, 7a
00153 Roma
Tel: +39-06-581-5378
Closed Sunday evenings,
all day Monday.

covering one whole side of the range; it was a spectacle similar to juggling. Desserts were simple: cakes purchased from a quality pasticceria, crème caramel, and my favorite—pears cooked with red wine and prunes. It's a classic winter dessert, simple to prepare and dramatic looking on a platter. Those who want a fancier dessert can serve it with sweetened mascarpone, ricotta, or whipped cream.

<table>
<tr><td>DESSERT</td><td>

PEARS WITH RED WINE

SERVES 4 TO 6

4–6 firm-fleshed pears
2–3 cups dry red wine
½ cup sugar
2 strips lemon zest
1 cinnamon stick (optional)
½–1 cup prunes, with or without pits

</td></tr>
</table>

Peel the pears with a vegetable peeler, leaving the stems as handles. Remove a slice off the bottom end of each so that the pears stand up. Place the pears in a heavy-bottomed nonreactive pan with a tight-fitting lid that is just large enough to hold them. Pour the wine over the pears, add the remaining ingredients, and bring to a boil over high heat. Lower the heat to very low, cover, and cook for 15 to 25 minutes or until tender when poked with a knife.

Remove the pears and prunes to a serving dish with a slotted spoon, raise the heat to high, and reduce the wine syrup until lightly thickened. Pour the syrup over the fruit and serve at room temperature, either plain or with lightly sweetened mascarpone, ricotta, or whipped cream.

* * *

Gennaro Esposito and Vittoria Aiello

*I*T WAS at the recommendation of my favorite Neapolitan restaurateur, Alfonso Mattozzi (page 174), that I first visited Torre del Saracino. When that recommendation was seconded by Salvatore de Gennaro (page 205), whose shop La Tradizione in nearby Seiano supplies the restaurant with cheese, Torre del Saracino vaulted to the top of my list of places to visit on my annual Christmas trip to the Sorrento peninsula with my husband Massimo.

This restaurant, owned by co-chefs and companions Gennaro Esposito and Vittoria Aiello, is next to a seventh-century Saracen watchtower overlooking the harbor of Marina di Seiano. The bay of Naples and Vesuvius are both visible in the distance. The menu combines wild seafood straight from the fisherman, local produce from a family farm, and super-fresh cow's milk ricotta and mozzarella from a nearby producer—all spotlighted in both classic and innovative dishes. Gennaro creates dishes like Parmigiano-style scabbard fish (*pesce bandiera*, a long, flat local fish); stubby pasta tubes (*paccheri*) dressed with seafood; and ricotta soup with red mullet fillet and sea urchin roe. Raw fish and seafood get just a drop of tasty sweet-and-sour lemon sauce. I wasn't sure how my fussy Tuscan husband, who insists on simplicity and extra virgin, and won't eat raw fish, would feel about Gennaro's cooking. Well, he skipped the raw seafood, but loved everything else as much as I did. We chatted with Gennaro after we finished Vittoria's walnut-stuffed figs drenched with chocolate sauce and Neapolitan baba with lemon custard and wild strawberries. As we left, Gennaro gave Massimo a big bag of local walnuts, the

TORRE DEL SARACINO
Via Torretta, 9
80069 Marina di Seiano, Vico Equense (NA)
Tel/Fax: +39-081-802-8555
info@torredelsaracino.it
www.torredelsaracino.com
Closed Sunday evening and Monday; closed January 20–February 12. All credit cards accepted.

perfect gift for my husband, who cracks nuts for dessert. Maybe that's why he's so enthusiastic about returning every Christmas.

Gennaro's recipe for lemon sauce is unlike anything I've ever tasted. Though I've shortened Gennaro's six-day procedure for candying the lemon zest that gives it its punch, it's still a two-day affair. Gennaro uses locally grown lemons that are sweeter than conventional citrus, but either way these zests are different—softer than purchased candied fruit and well worth the effort. The zest lasts indefinitely in the refrigerator, and once you've made it, the sauce is easy and quick to make. Gennaro serves a dab of sauce with raw seafood, but I use it with almost any simply prepared fish.

SAUCE

SWEET AND SOUR LEMON SAUCE

MAKES ABOUT ½ CUP SAUCE AND 1 CUP CANDIED ZEST

FOR THE CANDIED ZEST
2 organic or Meyer lemons
1 orange
6 tablespoons coarse sea salt
½ cup wildflower honey (Gennaro uses *millefiori*
    but any wildflower honey will do)
1 cup sugar

Peel the zest from two lemons in strips, leaving ¼-inch pulp attached to the zest. Peel the orange the same way. Put the zests in a bowl, toss with 2 tablespoons salt, add 1 cup water, and weight down with a small plate to keep zests submerged for 1 to 2 hours. Rinse and drain.

Bring 10 cups of water to a rolling boil. Add remaining 4 tablespoons salt and the zests, and when water returns to a rolling boil, remove from the heat and let zests cool completely in the salted water. Drain the zests.

Combine the honey, sugar, and 2¼ cups of fresh water in a small pot and bring to a simmer. Add the drained zest and cook over lowest heat, less than a simmer, for 40 minutes. Remove from the heat and let zest cool in syrup overnight.

The next day, bring the syrup back to a simmer, lower the heat, and cook for 1 hour. Remove from the heat and cool completely. Repeat the process one more time, cooking zest on the lowest heat for 30 minutes. Store zest in its syrup in a jar.

FOR THE SAUCE

3½ organic or Meyer lemons

2 tablespoons extra virgin olive oil

1 garlic clove, peeled

1 tablespoon minced celery

Fine sea salt

White pepper

3 tablespoons chopped candied lemon zest

   (or lemon and orange lemon if lemon is tart)

Trim three lemons with a knife, cutting the rind away down to the pulp. Section the lemon into wedges, cutting between the white connective membranes. Squeeze the juice from the remains of the lemons into a measuring cup and add the wedges. You should have around ½ cup. Squeeze the juice from the remaining ½ lemon and add it to the lemon wedges.

In a small saucepan, add the extra virgin and sauté the garlic and celery over medium heat until the celery barely begins to color. Add the lemon wedges and juice and cook, mashing the mixture with a wooden spoon, until the mixture is pulpy. Remove the garlic. Season the lemon mixture with salt and white pepper. If the sauce is too tart, add a spoonful or two of syrup from the candied zest.

Transfer lemon mixture to a blender and add candied zest. Emulsify until smooth.

Francesco Marrapese; Sergio and Stefano Massa

VILLA MASSA

Via Mortora S. Liborio, 126

80063 Piano di Sorrento (NA)

Tel: +39-081-750-6112

servizioclienti@villamassa.com

www.villamassa.com

SOLAGRI LEMONS

Coop. Solagri S.r.l.

Via S. Martino, 8

80065 S. Agnello (NA)

Tel: +39-081-877-2901

Fax: +39-081-877-2776

info@solagri.it

www.solagri.it

Visits by appointment only.

If you are traveling in the south,
contact Francesco:

Via Dei Platani, 24/F

80063 Piano di Sorrento (NA)

Cell: +39-338-338-7393

Fax: +39-081-532-3480

info@francescomarrapese.com

www.francescomarrapese.com

FRANCESCO MARRAPESE is handsome, smart, speaks colloquial English, and drives for his private car hire service on the Sorrento peninsula. When he drove my assistant Jenn, my sister (and illustrator) Suzanne, and me to a restaurant, we invited him to dine with us, which turned out to be a very smart move. He ordered wisely, drank modestly, and was fun to have at the table. His mother, a journalist, also does a little PR work, and Francesco suggested we visit a company she works with, Villa Massa, producers of quality limoncello, the lemon liqueur.

Which is how a group of chefs, food writers, restaurateurs from California, and I found ourselves, attired in white smocks and hair and shoe coverings, at the Villa Massa factory. Sergio and Stefano Massa macerate the zests of flavorful local organic lemons in alcohol, which is then filtered and combined with sugar syrup. In addition to the limoncello, we tasted walnut (*nocino*) and tangerine (*liquore di mandarino*) liqueurs, though I drew the line at the cream liqueurs. We also sampled Villa Massa's newest product, Dstill, a distilled—not infused—lemon spirit that is packaged in an attractive, slim, rectangular bottle; it's dry, citrusy, probably great for mixed drinks. My favorite product at Villa Massa is the lemon sorbet we were served after our tasting, made from the juice of the lemons whose peels go in the liqueurs. It's sold from an electric mini-truck (it can go into limited traffic zones where normal cars aren't allowed) patterned all over with lemons, oranges, and their leaves; in the warm months it can be found in the Sorrento, Amalfi, and Naples areas. If you can find organic lemons, try making your own limoncello; otherwise, search out the Massas' great products.

LIMONCELLO

MAKES AROUND 1 ¼ QUARTS

5 organic lemons, with untreated peels
2 cups grappa or vodka (in Italy you'd use 95 proof alcohol)
1 ½ cups sugar

Peel the lemons, removing only the zest (and none of the white pith) with a vegetable peeler. Place the zests in a large glass jar with the grappa, vodka, or alcohol. Cover the jar and macerate for 10 days in a cool, dark place—anywhere you'd keep wine. Filter the alcohol through a fine sieve or cheesecloth.

In a saucepan over medium heat, dissolve the sugar in 3 cups water to make a syrup. Add the syrup to the filtered alcohol and combine. Pour the liqueur into bottles and close with corks or stoppers. Let the limoncello "ripen" for two months in a cool, dark place. Serve cold (or even store in the freezer).

Franco, Graziella, and Pierpaolo Ruta

L'ANTICA DOLCERIA BONAJUTO

C.so Umberto I°, 159
97015 Modica (RG)
Tel/Fax: +39-0932-941-225
bonajuto@ragusaonline.com
www.bonajuto.it
Visits by appointment only.

DURING A VISIT to Sicily, my good pal and butcher Dario Cecchini and I went in search of the famous meat- and chocolate-stuffed pastries called 'mpanatigghi, a specialty of the village of Modica. When we spotted the Antica Dolceria di Bonajuto, we knew we were in the right place. The shop was lined with old-fashioned cupboards displaying cookies, quince-paste molds, objects used in Modica-style chocolate making, and attractively wrapped bars of chocolate and almond milk concentrate. Owner Franco Ruta explained that the chocolate came to Modica straight from the New World during its period of Spanish control, hence the same tools (stone pin and grinding surface with heat underneath) and style (sugar in crystals, not melted) as Mexico. "Check out the Museo Ibleo delle Arti e Traditizioni Populari if you want to see the way chocolate used to be made," suggested Franco. We went, and were thrilled by a huge collection of Sicilian carts and rooms dedicated to traditional crafts: basket weaver, wheel maker, carpenter, shoemaker, cheesemaker and, of course, a room devoted to chocolate making. A local guide led us through the rooms, explaining the exhibits. We questioned extensively and returned to Franco's shop filled with enthusiasm.

Franco introduced us to his wife Graziella and son Pierpaolo, who both help at the shop. They asked if we knew their friend, Modica homeboy Piero Selvaggio (owner of restaurants including Valentino in Los Angeles), and when we said that we did, Franco called L.A. to tell Piero about our visit. He was thrilled that we had made it to Modica and were charmed by Franco and his beautiful Baroque jewel of a town, not on most tourist itineraries of Sicily.

Because Franco, Graziella, and Pierpaolo's recipe for Sicilian hot chocolate is made without milk, which is not widely used in traditional Sicilian cooking, the pure flavor of chocolate shines. Tasting it is like discovering quality bittersweet chocolate after a life of Hershey's bars. Of course, Sicilian hot chocolate is best made with traditional Sicilian chocolate, which contains some wheat starch, which lightly thickens the hot chocolate. The finest is made by L'Antica Dolceria Bonajuto, which, though imported to the United States, is not easy to find. It is worth the search, and Pierpaolo has assured me that eventually it will be sold via their website.

SICILIAN HOT CHOCOLATE

MAKES 2 TO 4 DRINKS

1 bar (100 grams) Bonajuto chocolate; or 3½ ounces
    bittersweet chocolate plus 1 tablespoon wheat starch,
    and 2 tablespoons sugar
Ladyfingers (optional)

Chop the Bonajuto chocolate and melt it in 1½ cups water over low heat in a deep pot. If using bittersweet chocolate, combine the wheat starch and sugar, add ¼ cup water, and beat with a whisk to eliminate any lumps, then add 1¼ cups water and the chocolate. Remove from the heat and let the mixture rest for 10 minutes.

Reheat the chocolate until hot and whip over the heat until foamy, using a whisk or immersion mixer (traditionalists use a Sicilian tool like a Mexican molinillo, or wooden hot-chocolate beater). Pour into two coffee cups or four espresso cups and serve with ladyfingers, if desired, for dipping. Or eat with a spoon.

✳ ✳ ✳

ACKNOWLEDGMENTS

Thanks and *mille grazie* to:

Massimo, Max, and Giada, my family.

Suzanne, who painted a watercolor of Vito Santoro that inspired me, and made me realize I needed her illustrations for the book. She's one of my very best friends and lives around the corner.

Jennifer, who is stubborn, and made me write this book. She tracked down hundreds of friends, made lists, and e-mailed everything to Sharon, who tested recipes on Mark and Baba, with occasional advice from Josh. They're my second family.

Jay, my able agent; Susan, who bought the book; but most of all Pam and the team from Clarkson Potter, who believed in the watercolors as much as I did.

All my Italian friends who gave me recipes, and those who gave me recipes that I didn't have space for.

Alan, Alice, Annie, Barbara, Bill, Bruce, Carol, Catherine, Cathy, Corby, David, Francesca, George, Giudi, Herb, Jeff, Jo, Julian, Mario, Marvino, Nancy, Paolo, Paula, Piero, Stan, Teresa, Tom, Tony, Vicky, Vinnie, and especially the Wags.